BREAKING THROUGH MEXICO'S PAST

Frontispiece. Eduardo Matos and Davíd Carrasco posing with hats at the Bogart Hat Shop in Boulder, Colorado, during one of Eduardo's visits to the University of Colorado where he lectured on the new discoveries at the Templo Mayor, 1984.

BREAKING THROUGH
MEXICO'S PAST

Digging the Aztecs with
Eduardo Matos Moctezuma

DAVÍD CARRASCO

LEONARDO LÓPEZ LUJÁN

EDUARDO MATOS MOCTEZUMA

UNIVERSITY OF NEW MEXICO PRESS

ALBUQUERQUE

© 2007 by the University of New Mexico Press
All rights reserved. Published in 2007
Printed in the United States of America

12 11 10 09 08 07   1 2 3 4 5 6

LIBRARY OF CONGRESS CATALOGING-IN-PUBLICATION DATA

Carrasco, David.
Breaking through Mexico's past : digging the Aztecs with
    Eduardo Matos Moctezuma / Davíd Carrasco, Leonardo López Luján,
    Eduardo Matos Moctezuma.
        p. cm.
    ISBN-13: 978-0-8263-3831-0 (cloth : alk. paper)
    ISBN-10: 0-8263-3831-3 (cloth : alk. paper)
    1. Matos Moctezuma, Eduardo.
    2. Anthropologists—Mexico—Biography.
    3. Archaeologists—Mexico—Biography.
    4. Aztecs—Antiquities.
    5. Templo Mayor (Mexico City, Mexico)
    6. Mexico—Antiquities.
    I. López Luján, Leonardo.
    II. Matos Moctezuma, Eduardo.
    III. Title.
GN21.M38C37 2007
        301.092—dc22
        [B]
                                2006026326

DESIGN AND COMPOSITION: *Mina Yamashta*

Contents

Introduction

Eduardo Matos Moctezuma: Centaur at the Ready

"Digging into the soil of an ancient city,
the metal point of a pick encounters
a golden ornament, a sculptured stone,
an arrow, a fetish, a god of ambiguous form,
or the vast walls of a temple. My pick
is working in the soil of an unknown America.
May my poet's pick make harmonious sounds!
May it turn up gold and opals and rich fine stones,
a temple, or a broken statue!
And may the Muse divine the meaning of the hieroglyphics"
— Rubén Darío, "El Canto errante" (1907)

Following a concise and poetic meditation on archaeology as a journey into the past, his own aging and "el tiempo muerto," Eduardo Matos Moctezuma writes this compelling passage, characteristic of his attitude, near the end of this book, *Breaking Through Mexico's Past*,

El viaje que hoy emprenderemos nos permitirá dos cosas: remontarnos varios siglos atrás en esa moderna máquina del tiempo que es la arqueología, pues al arqueólogo también le es dado recuperar el tiempo ido por medio de las excavaciones y, además, llegar al mundo de los muertos, en donde encontraremos los rostros que fueron y que nos ven, con ojos pétreos, a través del tiempo mismo . . .

Estoy listo . . .

Those of us who know and love him also know that in a unique and very creative way Eduardo has always been *listo*, i.e., alert, ready, focused, mentally dexterous in the face of his life's challenges and opportunities.

Eduardo, more than any other archaeologist of our time, has effectively navigated the challenges, surprises, vicissitudes, and opportunities of Mexico's astonishing archaeological world and he has aided his countrymen and the wider world in grasping, and digging into, in Darío's words, the profounder cultural and political meanings of "an ancient city" in Mesoamerica. On a personal level, Eduardo received from his family the gift of personal *voluntad* or willpower, which he cultivated by facing, with special intensity and intelligence, the five major challenges of his life, what he calls "los cinco rompimientos del centauro." As these pages show this voluntad consists of a powerful combination of deep curiosity and willpower. On the one hand, from early in childhood he demonstrated an intense desire to more fully understand the workings of the cosmos he lived in, manifested in natural events, religious and secular schools, political revolutions, the lives of women, the lives and death of children, encounters with "golden ornaments, sculptured stones," and gods "of ambiguous form." On the other hand and often in the face of obstacles that would have defeated most of us, he wielded an effective drive to make parts of that world work to his benefit and to the benefit of his scientific colleagues and even his country's cultural identity. The centerpiece of this journey through the labyrinth of the *cinco rompimientos* was, as in Darío's poem, "the vast walls of a temple" in the soil of an unknown Mexico, i.e., his masterful excavation of the Aztec Great Temple. In the astonishing successes of this excavation, symbolically located at the axis of Mexico City's colonial district, Eduardo helped to renovate Mexico's cultural and ceremonial place of *orientatio*, the Zócalo of the city and the Zócalo of the Mexican imagination, whose roots dig back to the Aztec empire when other Moctezumas walked the land.

His near-mythic stature in Mexico is reflected in the Spanish subtitle of this book, *Los rompimientos del centauro*—of which they are five—because this fivefold pattern puts his autobiography in tune with the five-part cosmogram imprinted on the Aztec Calendar Stone and in so many Mesoamerican myths. It is appropriate for us to think of his life, career, loves, losses, and extraordinary scientific and cultural achievements with a tinge of Mexican mythology. After all, here is man who becomes a kind of culture hero in his country but whose life story is full of strange themes, like the gods of Mexico: themes of great creativity (weaving the disciplines and individuals of *Proyecto Templo Mayor* into a creative team), marginality (childhood outside of Mexico in Panama, Venezuela), physical impairment (*tartamudo* [stuttering], which he overcomes), painful ruptures (broken relationships, the loss of a beloved child, renunciation of high positions, fascinations with death), journeys to other worlds (China, Australia, United States, Europe, through Chiapanec jungles and into the Aztec world beneath Mexico City's cathedral), and artistic powers (sculptor, poet, teacher, director, museum designer, universal Mexican). Eduardo in a unique way has become one of Mexico's culture heroes, a visionary, and as in the poem by Darío, he helps "divine the meaning of the hieroglyphics," the sacred signs of Tenochtitlan in particular and Mesoamerica in general. His extraordinary combination of scientific work, poetic spirit, and political savvy is reflected in the mythological animal that he has chosen to characterize himself by: the centaur, the mythical man-horse whose complex powers of speed, intelligence, virility, strength, cunning, and a capacity to play the trickster distinguished him from others in the Greek pantheon.[1]

---

1. The best of the centaurs was Chiron, known for his exceptional goodness and wisdom, which he passed on as a tutor to a number of famous Greek heroes including the great Achilles.

Meeting and interviewing Eduardo

These interviews into his life began in 1990 when Eduardo's achievements at the Aztec Great Temple had attracted international acclaim and we wanted to understand the sources and even secrets of his creativity. We hoped that by asking him about his childhood, family history, most important relationships, inner struggles, education, personal chemistry, and the shape of his intellect we could help develop a narrative that would reveal how Eduardo came to accomplish so much for himself, archaeology, and for Mexico. In particular we wanted to comprehend better what had prepared him to take on and succeed at the truly monumental Proyecto Templo Mayor, which had a very large series of excavation, publication, conference, public presentation, and media projects associated with it. The reader of these pages will discover the personal, professional, and poetic keys that unlock the secrets of his extraordinary development as a scientist and a culture hero. The first interviews were carried out over a ten-year period by Davíd Carrasco in Mexico City; Boulder, Colorado; and at Princeton University. From the beginning, Eduardo showed willingness and even a fascination with telling his life story and we both had the impression that he was discovering elements and connections of his past life as well as rediscovering events, motives, and deeper issues in his work, family, friendships, and rise to fame. At a certain stage in the narration process, Carrasco realized that there were questions that needed to be asked about Eduardo's archaeological education and the profound achievements at the Templo Mayor that he, Carrasco, did not know how to ask. He turned to Leonardo López Luján who had worked closely with Eduardo at Proyecto Templo Mayor during more than twenty years and who directed the excavation of the House of Eagles at the sacred precinct of Tenochtitlan. López Luján carried out, together with Carrasco as well as on his own, a series of interviews that enriched the overall narrative of Eduardo's life and career.

The preparation of the Spanish manuscript for this book, as well as the overall organization of both the Spanish and English versions, was significantly enhanced by the Mexican linguist and scholar of bilingual acquisition, Dra. María Luisa Parra of Boston University.

Carrasco first heard of Eduardo when he was studying with Pedro Armillas, the incomparable Spaniard who helped revitalize Mexican archaeology in the decades immediately following the Spanish Civil War. Armillas was teaching anthropology at the University of Illinois, Circle Campus and he became Carrasco's tutor on many archaeological topics in Mesoamerica, and especially in relation to the archaeology of the Feathered Serpent cult in central Mexico. When Carrasco needed to do a field trip to visit the Feathered Serpent cities in central Mexico, Armillas wrote him a generous letter of intro-duction to "my excellent student, Eduardo Matos" in Mexico. He spoke to Carrasco of Eduardo and his generation of archaeologists with pride and hope that new discoveries and understandings would continue to be forthcoming in the study of Mesoamerican history and society. Today's scholars have become aware of how important Armillas is for contemporary archaeological knowledge. In many essays and books, we find pointed references to how Armillas's vision of ecological and historical turning points, material conditions, and social organization had proved fundamental to studies and models of Mesoamerican history. Eric Wolf said it best in his dedication of the book *Sixteenth Century Mexico* when he wrote "To Pedro Armillas, who led the way." Having a sponsor like Armillas was a dream come true for Carrasco, in part, because he led his student into the office, work, and life of Eduardo Matos Moctezuma, who at that time was serving as director of Pre-hispanic Monuments at the Instituto Nacional de Antropología e Historia (INAH). Still wet behind the ears while completing his dissertation on Quetzalcóatl and the irony of empire, Carrasco met Eduardo in 1976 in his office in Mexico City. After reading Armillas's letter introducing a Chicano historian of religions who had worked with Mircea Eliade and Paul Wheatley at the University of Chicago, Eduardo made the first of a lifelong series of generous gestures in Davíd's direction by writing him letters of introduction to the *guardianes* of archaeological zones at Xochicalco, Teotihuacan, and Tula and by giving his visitor an autographed copy of his recently published *Muerte a filo de obsidiana*. Carrasco has always felt blessed that Pedro Armillas put him in contact with Eduardo and it was only several years later that Davíd came to realize how deeply Armillas was held in respect by Eduardo and other Mexican archaeologists. Symbolically, the very first photograph inside Eduardo's edited volume, *Descubridores del pasado en Mesoamérica*, is of Pedro Armillas and José García Payón examining a column with the image of *13 Conejo* in El Tajín.

López Luján began to work with Eduardo as a teenaged novice or "slave"—the name archaeologists affectionately use for students and anyone working for free—in the summer of 1980 when he was sixteen years old. The previous year López Luján had visited the site of the Great Temple for the first time and was awakened to the cultural significance and even magic of archaeological work when he viewed the Coyolxauhqui stone in situ and witnessed other *ofrendas* and astonishing pieces of Aztec sculpture. Having previously read books on major archaeological discoveries and washed Maya shards for Alberto Ruz—the discoverer of King Pakal's tomb—Leonardo's visits to the Templo Mayor stimulated him to ask Eduardo for a chance to work at the site and "learn by doing" archaeology. Eduardo replied, "Come tomorrow at 8:00 a.m. to the Great Temple. You know how to get there." During the following years, López Luján became part of the expert team of scientists who witnessed a florescence of Aztec archaeology as a result of the astonishingly rich discoveries that were being made almost daily. His working relationship with the team and especially with Eduardo deepened until he was eighteen, when he realized that he had found his life's vocation. López Luján combined his fieldwork with university studies that culminated in his Ph.D. in Aztec archaeology from the University of Paris in 1998. Over the years a profound collaboration with Eduardo developed as López Luján participated in and witnessed the cultural and archaeological *renovatio* at the Templo Mayor brought about by the combination of the archaeological dig and the establishment and educational programs of the Museo Templo Mayor.

Lineages and life

Eduardo's style of being "ready" and his dedication to the full range of archaeology's cultural significance can be seen in the following story. Several years ago, he was chosen to receive the inaugural "H. B. Nicholson Award for Excellence in Mesoamerican Studies" from Harvard's Peabody Museum of Archaeology and Ethnology. The ceremonial dinner was held during a Mesoamerican Archive conference and many of Eduardo's longtime colleagues were on hand, including the inimitable H. B. Nicholson himself, who spoke eloquently and with great affection about Eduardo's singular contributions. As the minutes ticked down to the start of the dinner in the North American Indian Hall where several astonishing Tinglit totem poles stood sentry over the dinner guests, Eduardo suddenly asked Carrasco to walk with him up the back stairway of the museum. Earlier in the day, while on the way to a meeting, he briefly noticed the names of distinguished Harvard anthropologists, long deceased, on the doors of their old offices. Now, as he was about to receive this honor from Harvard and filled with emotion tinged with great respect for the scientific tradition in which he worked and lived, he felt an urge to gaze on those names, symbolically showing his respect before receiving the H. B. Nicholson medal. Out through the narrow hallway they went past the caterers who were putting the last preparatory touches on the meal. Then, up the stairs to doors that had these names and dates on them.

A. M. Tozzer 1902–1954
A. V. Kidder 1914–1921
C. Kluckhohn 1960–
H. J. Spinden 1921–1929
G. R. Willey 1950–2002
W. L. Fash 1995–

After visiting the two floors where these names were painted on office doors, Eduardo stopped and stared, smiled slightly in admiration, shook his shoulders and head as though to release emotion and said "These men made great contributions to our knowledge. I feel honored to be associated with them. Ahora me siento listo para recibir la Medalla Nicholson (Now I feel ready to accept the Nicholson Medal)." And so he did at a joyous dinner with kudos filling the air.

This little journey with Matos confirmed for Carrasco something he had suspected. Eduardo has a genius for leadership and anthropological interpretation but he understands himself and his many honors as part of lineages which endowed him with knowledge, mysteries, and probing questions by great teachers. Matos saw himself as a link in an honorable chain that went back in one direction to and through the names on those doors and forward in another direction toward the archaeologists, poets, and sculptors yet to come. Davíd was moved by Eduardo's humility and pride of lineage which, while centered in Mexican achievements, reaches beyond them to those who helped Mesoamerica's diverse peoples find places in our science, in our books, and in our hearts.

This same desire of wanting to know and celebrate the human faces of archaeology can be seen in his curated show and book *Descubridores del pasado en Mesoamérica,* a photographic and narrative masterpiece of Mesoamerica's historical archaeology. This passage about Eduardo in Dolores Béistegui de Robles's "Preámbulo" to the book illustrates our point. She writes

En una conversación con Eduardo Matos sobre arqueología, le pregunté acerca de los hombres que se han dedicado a esta ciencia y de la importancia de sus hallazgos para el conocimiento de nuestro pasado. La respuesta del profesor Matos fue tan apasionada y enriquecedora, que concluimos que el tema de esa conversación debía ser abordado en una magna exposición.

Reading the Chronology of *Breaking Through Mexico's Past* results in a series of surprises as the multi-country, multi-narrative story of his life is mapped for us. Although Eduardo was born in Mexico in 1940, his father was a diplomat from the Dominican Republic, while his mother, Edith Moctezuma Barreda, was Mexican. This diversity led to another as he lived the first ten years of his life outside of Mexico (traveling to Panama during his first year of life on the ship "América") in Panama, Venezuela, Honduras, and the Dominican Republic while his father served with distinction in the Dominican diplomatic corps. As a five-year-old he witnessed the physical assault by Venezuelans on his home i.e., the Dominican embassy in Caracas. As a ten- to twelve-year-old, his sense of Latin American political revolt intensified when his father renounced his position as ambassador to Honduras in protest against the "tirano dominicano Rafael Trujillo Molina." One can suggest that the young Eduardo, witnessing these dangerous upheavals from the ambassador's residences, developed his historical vision of *rompimientos* as well as an insight that personal and political will, or *voluntad*, was an effective instrument of survival and leadership. Upon returning to Mexico in 1952, Eduardo continued his education in religious schools (it had been the *Lasallistas* in Panama; in Mexico it was the Jesuits and Augustinians) and it was here that he encountered his first rompimiento, his struggle with the existence or non-existence of God. The reader will see that this crisis was a crucial turning point

in his life which set a pattern for his subsequent, powerful transformations and the creative breaks and restorations of his life. We
see Eduardo and his struggle for creativity during his student years
at the Escuela Nacional de Antropología e Historia and discover
his profound and humorous encounter with the work of Rilke, his
love of many women, his fascination with the Cuban revolution,
and his long-standing ties to many of Mexico's great archaeologists and teachers. We learn from him as he maps the archaeological
currents of the second half of the twentieth century and manages
the emergence of Coyolxauqui from her tomb of nearly 500 years.
We hold on tight as he recalls his breaks in his family and per-
forms as the Prince of Persia, without his much needed glasses, in an
opera in Mexico City. We discover how he travelled the world and
introduced the astonishing discoveries about the Aztec civilization
to Europe and Asia. In this inspiring and often humorous narrative we discover not only the details and crucial events of his life,
but we also encounter essential aspects of all our lives—erotic love
and professional friendships, fear of the known and the unknown,
and the many faces of death. Through it all we see Matos weaving
threads of renewal, reinvention, and revitalization. In partial answer
to the large question posed above "what had 'prepared' him to take
on and succeed at the truly monumental *Proyecto Templo Mayor?*"
readers will discover that Eduardo's career is in no way limited or
confined to his expert management of the Templo Mayor excavation and *Museo del Templo Mayor*. His determination to become a
first-rate archeologist and contribute significantly and in innovative
ways to Mexico's scientific recovery of its civilizational past led him
to work strenuously under the guidance of Mexico's superb anthropological faculties and in some of Mesoamerica's most interesting
archeological cities. The diversity of these efforts is evident in his
archaeology at Bonampak, Comalcalco, and Malpaso in the Maya
area, and at Cholula, Tula, Teotihuacan, Tenochtitlan, and Tlatelolco

in central Mexico. His general vision of Mesoamerican archaeology was also nurtured by a variety of teachers who constitute the Archaeology All Stars, including José Luis Lorenzo, Calixta Guiteras Holmes, Richard S. MacNeish, Román Piña Chan, Jorge R. Acosta, Pedro Armillas, Francisco González Rul, Bodo Spranz, and Ignacio Bernal, among others. Here we see a key to his ritual gesture of respect that evening at Harvard's Peabody Museum.

When Octavio Paz passed away he was referred as a "universal Mexican" because of the extraordinary reach of his writings, his worldwide travels, and his winning the Nobel Prize in Literature. In a different way, Eduardo Matos Moctezuma is a "universal Mexican" because he led scores of scientists, writers, journalists, and the citizens of Mexico and other countries through "la ventana del tiempo" (the window of time) into a new appreciation of the Mesoamerican universe as it was constructed, ritualized, lived daily, and imagined by the millions of people who built the first cities in the New World. As the final chapters in this book show, the Aztecs conquered the world through the still ongoing exhibitions, lectures, honors, and awards associated with his name and unique achievements. He said "estoy listo" meaning "I'm ready," but he has also said in his life's work, always tinged with his special sense of humor, "soy listo," which with the alternative verb form can mean "I'm clever" or in English vernacular can be translated "I'm at the ready" or "I've got it covered—you can count on me." We have counted on him so much in our careers and he has not only been ready, he has been productive, empathic, effective, and has revitalized what he has touched. We give him the last word and perhaps his symbol, the symbol of his life and achievements, is the *caracol* (caracole, or conch shell) with its revitalizing energy, its lines both taut with potential force and flowing into a vital beauty. He writes of the caracol this way in his poem "El Rostro de la vida . . . y de la muerte":

El caracol es símbolo de vida.

El artista que lo creó hizo no sólo vida a través de la forma,

sino que unió volumen y ritmo y logró,

con líneas que se desparraman suavemente,

el movimiento constante y eterno del símbolo vital.

—Davíd Carrasco and Leonardo López Luján

CHAPTER ONE

Childhood

D: EDUARDO MATOS MOCTEZUMA, your surname is rather uncommon, but very significant. Talk to us about the origin of your name and give us some insight into the interest it arouses in other people.

E: Well, the surname Moctezuma comes from my mother's side of the family. My mother, Edith Moctezuma Barreda, was from the state of Puebla in Mexico, and she claimed to be a descendant of the emperor. Really, my siblings and I didn't pay much attention to her claim, but I could tell, even as a child, that she took it very seriously. She used to tell us the story of one of the viceroys who governed New Spain who had the titles of Count of Moctezuma y Tula, Viscount of Ilucan. One day this viceroy was riding horseback down the street, when his horse stumbled, and he was thrown to the ground. A man who was nearby helped him to his feet, and the viceroy told him, "Thank you. Since you have helped me, you may come to the viceregal palace and ask me for a reward."

The man went to the palace and requested of the viceroy that his titles be recognized, since his surname was Moctezuma and he was from the state of Puebla. The viceroy then sent two priests to investigate whether his name was really Moctezuma, and to find out what the local people thought of him. They returned and reported that he was very much respected in that place and that, in fact, he was considered to be a descendant of the emperor. I don't really know whether my mother invented this tale or whether it was true, but that is what she told us. One day she even showed us a coat of arms painted by a friend that she said was the coat of arms of the Moctezuma family, with an eagle, an ocelot or jaguar, and three vertical bands. She said this was the coat of arms of the Moctezuma family. My father didn't take it very seriously; instead he used to joke about my mother's notions, calling her "her Ladyship, the Marchioness of Moctezuma." For me, really, it hasn't been important to find out whether I'm a descendant of the emperor or not, but I understand that sometimes the question does arouse a lot of interest in others. Recently I was in Italy, and the central issue for the reporters and the obligatory question was whether I was a descendant of the emperor.

D: Maybe because you excavated the temple of Moctezuma.

E: Exactly. It's true that one writer, Gustavo Sainz, dedicated his book *Fantasmas aztecas* to me, and it deals with my life and the relationship of my surname to my having excavated the Templo Mayor of the Aztecs. But to get back to the Italian reporters—on my last visit, just like the one I made five years ago, the relationship between my surname and the emperor was always the subject of questions. At first I answered that I really didn't know whether I was a descendant or not. But faced with the insistent questioning, I finally answered yes, yes, I was a descendant of the emperor. So they were quite pleased and published in the newspapers, "A descendant of the Aztec emperor is here. . . ."

First steps: Panama and Venezuela

D: The story about your surname is interesting because it shows that there was a certain direction in your life, although it may not always have been conscious. It is almost unbelievable that it would be a Moctezuma who would excavate the temple of Moctezuma. But to return to your childhood, tell us some of your experiences from that time and your youth which opened your mind to the world of the past, or to archaeology, for example.

E: Look, this is a very interesting question. First let me tell you this: my father, Rafael Matos Díaz, was a diplomat, and not a Mexican—he was from the Dominican Republic. I was born in Mexico but when I was around six months old we moved to Panama on account of my father's diplomatic career. We were in Panama from 1941 to 1943. Later we went to Venezuela, where my father's responsibilities took him. One of my earliest childhood memories is of Venezuela, because I had a very traumatic experience there. It happened that during those years the Venezuelan government was overthrown. We lived in the Embassy of the Dominican Republic. I remember that we were at home the day of the *coup d'état*. The streets were a scene of total chaos and battle, and some people were attempting to take over the embassy where we were. My grandmother, María Barreda de Moctezuma, who was a very energetic, strong person, took charge of my older brother Rafael, my younger sister María Fernanda, and myself and moved us from the embassy to the home of some neighbors. We hid there until the army came and removed the people who had taken over the embassy.

We went back to our home, and the impression it made on me was tremendous, because everything was ruined, completely destroyed. My mother's grand piano was thrown halfway down the stairs with a leg broken off. The curtains were torn down, everything was ripped up and destroyed by the people who had come in. They stole my mother's silverware, the cushions, everything. Diplomatic relations between Venezuela and the Dominican Republic were broken off.

D: How did the crisis impact the next stage of your life?

E: We went to live at the Mexican embassy, because my mother and her children were Mexican. From there we traveled to Santo Domingo, where we stayed for some time, more than a year. Around 1945 or 1946 they sent my father back to Panama as ambassador.

And here my worldview began to expand. I was a child of six or seven and I remember that my mother was reading us Charles Darwin's *Origin of Species* when my brother and I went to bed. I mention this because my mother was a very devout Catholic, and still she would read the entire evolutionist position of this author to her little children. I don't believe this influenced me to dedicate myself later to the study of the past, but at least I remember that it was very interesting to hear how the monkey was gradually transformed into man. I don't know whether my mother read it to us so that we would learn this point of view or just to make us sleep.

D: One of the themes you mentioned that might bear some relation to your career in archaeology is that when you were a child and experienced that revolution in Venezuela you saw your house in ruins. You've studied many ruins in your life. In conjunction with the theories of Darwin, maybe at some level in your mind there has been a subconscious connection with that childhood episode. How old were you when those events took place?

E: I was very young, really. I mentioned, for example, that the attack or the destruction of our house happened when I was four years old, and the reading of Darwin when I was seven or eight.

D: The combination of revolution and Darwin is interesting. I also have the impression that you had experiences of other worlds from an early age: Venezuela, Santo Domingo, Panama . . . And archaeology is another world: the world of the past. You were prepared, perhaps, at a subconscious level. You were ready to enter other worlds, to discover ruins and treasures.

E: Possibly. I remember that as a child in Panama I thought about discovering a treasure, and I don't think it was just me, but probably all children have this fantasy. I remember at the side of the embassy there was a vacant field and some friends and I took little boxes with a few coins in them and hid them there, but really more with the idea that they were treasures.

D: Tell us a little about your life in Panama. What memories do you have of that country and the time you lived there?

E: Panama has always stayed with me. We lived there more or less from the time I was five until I was ten. So we lived five years in Panama and it was a place I really liked. Although I was young. I remember those good times in my childhood. It was extremely hot and perhaps, as you were saying, I don't know if something remained from it in my subconscious. It could be.

D: Another very famous Mexican, Carlos Fuentes, was born and raised for some years in that country. Is there a story about you and Carlos?

E: Well yes, and this is an odd thing. I didn't know that Carlos Fuentes was also the son of a diplomat, and that he had been in some of those countries. One day not long ago, I turned on the television and was watching a program already in progress. They were saying that this person is the son of a diplomat and has lived in Panama and in such and such a country and I thought: they're talking about me, that's my biography. And then they identified the person as Carlos Fuentes, so I found out that Carlos's life had a number of aspects that paralleled my early life.

D: As we know in Panama there is a large presence of the United States, and not always of a friendly sort. It is a military presence and there are often conflicts. What were your first impressions of the United States and its relations with Latin America?

E: I remember that as diplomats we could enter the Canal Zone, that is, the American zone. We could even go to a place where we could swim, a beach called Fort Amador, exclusively for the American Army. To me it was like entering another world for short periods. There was a sort of barrier that you passed at the beach and you came to another world.

To begin with, I didn't understand anything because they spoke another language. I remember that we used to go to swim there and the car had to pass through a guard post manned by American MPs. My mother would take out a little card to show them, and there was this word I really liked a lot: "OK." When the soldier said "OK" we went through to swim there. But Panama was always a slightly negative world of experience for me because my mother, wanting us to learn English, enrolled us in an American school in the Canal Zone during our vacations. My brother and I went to this school where we didn't understand anything. The children, quite naturally, looked at us with indifference, there was no communication, we didn't play together. I remember during my first year going into the classroom, sitting at a desk, and them giving me a sheet of paper that I couldn't understand or read; I felt really small. I don't know if that is why I have always felt a certain barrier with the English language. Maybe my reaction to English was caused by the pressure my mother exerted in putting us in that school. In reality we were not at all integrated into that world. I always saw this as a negative memory, as the experience of a child who was isolated, who couldn't talk with the other children, who was alone without the possibility of any form of communication. But in general I did enjoy Panama a lot. I studied the first years of primary school there in a religious school of the La Salle Brothers, called Miramar. I became so fond of those brothers of the religious order of San Juan Bautista de la Salle that years later when I returned to Mexico, I wanted to become a La Salle Brother.

D: Hearing your stories, I have the impression that sadness is a recurring theme of your childhood and youth. Is that true?

E: You're right. One time I went to a friend who is a psychoanalyst and he asked me: Eduardo, tell me, what are your earliest memories, the first memories that you can recall?

Then I told him that the earliest one, probably the oldest one, was when I was about two years old and lived in Panama. It was really just an image of something that fell, like a doll or a teddy bear, something like that, and I cried a lot. It's just an isolated memory. Later there are others like the experience I told you about in the embassy in Venezuela. I mean, a child who sees his home attacked and destroyed, things broken, who has to flee running to a nearby house. It was a harsh experience. I remember an interesting thing. The house they attacked, the embassy in Venezuela, was very large. It was called "Quinta Castillet." This mansion had maybe four floors, and I remember that it was so large that we didn't use the top floor. And there was a chest up there that seemed to me like a coffin or a sarcophagus. I would climb the stairs fearfully and peek at that chest and go back down terrified. I also remember that the house had a large garden on all four sides, where there were huge rats. I don't know if they seemed huge to me because I was very small and I experienced them as larger than they really were, but they were rats. When I told my psychoanalyst about this, he asked me:

"Well, and what conclusion do you draw from these memories?"

I answered: "Well, they are just experiences, I don't know."

He told me: "No, they are all unhappy memories. You haven't told me one memory where you were laughing."

This realization made a lasting impression on me. I have these early memories that are mostly negative, and not a moment of laughter or happiness, although of course those lighthearted moments must also have happened.

D: Your childhood stories link ruins, broken objects, and travel to diplomatic posts with your family. And it seems to me that your work as an archaeologist is also a sort of diplomatic career, since you are a person who travels a lot, going to Venezuela, Europe, the United States, and other countries very successfully. This brings your father to mind. What was the influence, the relationship you had with your father?

E: Well, my father was a very quiet person, pretty introverted, I think. He didn't touch us. We saw that he loved us by his expressions, but I remember that he practically never touched us, neither me nor my siblings. Even so, he did show us affection and love. That was very important. But as to what you were asking about, I have always had the notion of being a diplomat. That is, I have always thought of someday having a post of that type, traveling and representing my country. Perhaps because I lived in that environment as a child. Although at times I saw that it was a superficial environment, a little false because you lived two or three years in a country, and then they transferred you and there was not time enough to make friends, or you lost them. Still, I have always found it attractive. In fact, my sister just received a diplomatic post, so maybe she also has something of that feeling.

There is another important thing about my father: he was a historian. He didn't study history formally, but he was a very enlightened, well-educated man who knew a great deal about literature and history, and who wrote very well. I remember sometimes he would read to us at meals, at dinner, for example, about illustrious Dominicans, like Pedro Henríquez Ureña. Henríquez Ureña was very important, even in Mexico, during the first decades of this century and Alfonso

Reyes acknowledged him as a master. He is a person who interested me greatly as well, and I have written about him. My father read us these paragraphs or details about Dominican history. Although I may not have realized it at the time, and sometimes even made faces when my father started to read something to us, it seems possible that some of it stayed with me. So you can imagine—I grew up between Darwin and my father's readings. Around that time also my father bought us various books which I read enthusiastically. For example, *Amadís de Gaula, Cuentos armoricanos, La canción de Rolando* . . . Who could have guessed that many years later I would be writing about the *Doce Pares de Francia*, a dance which is danced in the Mexican state of Puebla, and which deals precisely with Charlemagne and his battle in Roncesvalles, which is recorded in the *Song of Roland* . . . !

The return to Mexico: searching for willpower

D: Can you recall any other books from your youth that made a great impression on you and contributed to your personal and professional development? Who were your favorite authors?

E: Here we enter into an area that is very important in my life. On returning to Mexico, coming from Honduras where my father had been transferred as ambassador, I began, around the age of twelve or thirteen, to feel the desire to become a monk, to be one of the Brothers of La Salle with whom I had studied in Panama. And I began to live a very ascetic life and read many lives of saints, Saint Luis Gonzaga, Saint Isabel of Hungary, their lives. There was a sort of comic book published in Mexico called *Vidas ejemplares*. It was about the lives of saints. I read them all. Of course this had a strong influence on an adolescent only thirteen years old who wanted to be a monk. Before we returned to Mexico, in Honduras, my father gave me a book which I saved for a long time. It was called *Hacia las cumbres*. I liked the title, and the cover showed a couple climbing high up on a mountain. I was enchanted by the phrase "Toward the summits" and the image of ascent to a higher level of reality. It was like a call to excel and overcome every difficulty. Around that time, inspired by the title I wrote these verses:

Visionary, steer your craft well,
Let the sea not alter your course.
Steer your ship toward the arcane
Steer ever toward the heights

This was a key moment in my life which I think was decisive, because I decided then that if I wanted to be a monk, I had to be one for real. That meant achieving sainthood. So what did I do? I imposed the obligation on myself of making twenty sacrifices each day. I made a little form in a notebook where I recorded, day by day, twenty sacrifices, and if I reached a certain number of years without failing, I would become a saint. I would achieve sainthood. What were these sacrifices? They were, for example, if I arrived at the school out of breath from running and I wanted water, I would not drink. I would hold out for an hour even if I was dying of thirst. Only then would I drink water. And I would record it with a mark. I had to do twenty things like that. Another example: around that time I was beginning to experience sexual awakening, at thirteen or fourteen. If a pretty girl with nice legs walked by, I would control myself and not turn to look at her. That was another sacrifice, another mark. I went to Mass almost daily, that was another. I prayed the Rosary at least four or five times a day; each one was another little mark. I came to do some frankly disgusting things. For example, I had a dog that I really loved, and he would be enjoying himself, chewing one of his bones. Then I would come and I would take it from him and lick it; that was another sacrifice. But at that time, in spite of the effort involved in these sacrifices, I was unaware that something really important was developing inside me: willpower, a strong willpower and tremendous self-control. I believe that the self-control which I was developing at that time turned out to be very significant later on a number of occasions.

One day something very curious happened, which I still can't explain. I think what I'm going to tell you was a highly unusual coincidence; I don't believe in miracles. But when I relate it, many people say, "Yes, that happened because of your willpower." I remember that we were in secondary school in Mexico. I would have been around fourteen years old, and in a biology class they had asked us to go out and collect some specimens—some insects or plant specimens. Two friends and I planned to go on foot to a far away place, a ravine. As we were about to depart from the school, my friends said,

"Listen, we had better not go, because look at the sky. It's going to rain. It's going to take us an hour to get there and an hour to come back, and there's going to be a huge thunderstorm and we're going to get soaked."

And I replied, with absolute certainty,

"No, no it's not going to rain. Come on, let's go. I promise it's not going to rain."

So we left and I kept praying and saying it wouldn't rain. We got to the place and collected the insects and started back. By then the sky was ready to break open, with huge, dark clouds. My friends kept saying: "Let's hurry! This is impossible. It's going to rain!"

And I told them: "No, don't worry. There's no problem. It's not going to rain."

We walked for an hour going back and went into the school. And I'm telling you, the moment we walked through the door into the school there was a cloudburst. I was really astonished and I kept praying. I believe it was a coincidence. Other people say, "No, it was your strength of will." Well, I don't know, but I certainly remember that it made a strong impression on me because it was very odd, a very notable occurrence.

D: That's an interesting story, not only for its religious dimension, but also from the point of view of your willpower. Because right up to the present you have always had self-confidence and a strength of will that have helped you throughout your career. Could we go back for a moment to your wanting to attain sainthood? One of your discoveries with respect to saints was the power of sacrifice. What other discoveries did you make during those years when you were reading the lives of saints? Anything comic or profound, because those lives are very strange.

E: Reading those lives changed me. I would say they stimulated me more in terms of the religious attitude I held at that time. My life was permeated with religious things. I'll tell you another interesting anecdote. When I was in the second year of high school I studied at Alonso de la Veracruz, a school run by Augustine friars. One of the teachers asked a friend and I if we wanted to go visit a Benedictine monastery. Well, of course, because I was in that religious frame of mind, I was delighted. We planned a stay at the monastery that was near Cuernavaca. We would also take advantage of our visits to study for an exam. My father took the two of us, my friend, who was Guatemalan, and I. We arrived at the monastery and one of the Benedictine monks greeted us. I was really pleased to have an opportunity to see what that experience was like. I remember that the monk told my father: Fine, don't worry. They'll be here. Give your son your blessing.

My father, who was never very religious, didn't know what to do. His blessing? How? He didn't know. I remember that all he did was sort of touch my nose with his hand. I think the monk must have wondered, "What was that?" My father left and we stayed at the monastery for a week. During that week we lived the life of the monks, getting up at four in the morning, going to Mass, hearing the Gregorian chants they sang. I remember that one day the Prior of the monastery asked to see us separately. I went into his cell and he began to ask me questions. He was Brother Gregorio Lemercier. He was very famous because he introduced psychoanalysis into the monastery and created an enormous problem for the Church. He was a tremendously intelligent man, a Belgian, who had founded this monastery. What really impressed me was seeing his shelves of books from floor to ceiling, full of books of all kinds. He had books on Marxism, on Mao, on Lenin, on Stalin. He had books on the lives of saints, books about the Pope, on the history of the Church. In other words, he was a very broad-minded, remarkable fellow. I remember we started talking and he gave me a book to read. It was called *The Stars Look Down*. He told me, "Read it and come back in three days so we can discuss it." I was very much impressed with Father Gregorio, and admired him a great deal. I didn't see him again afterward, I only heard about his conflict with the church and how he left the priesthood precisely because of his struggle against that reactionary aspect of the church. He wanted to introduce psychoanalysis into the church so that the monks would be psychoanalyzed and have a true vocation, and not be there because of some other type of personal problem.

D: What seems interesting here is your discovery of sacred spaces, although the religious power of this particular sacred space is rather complicated. It contained messages about psychoanalysis, books on Marxism, and an innovative priest. You have mentioned psychoanalysis several times. Do you think that psychoanalysis somehow cures a person?

E: Well, I believe that psychoanalysis can help a person with certain kinds of problems. It depends also on the person seeking self-understanding. And yet, on the other hand, I see relatives and friends who sometimes have spent years and years and have become so dependent on it that they can't get out of it. So I think that psychoanalysis can sometimes have a negative result.

D: Have you had the experience of being cured by psychoanalysis?

E: I had a very interesting "cure." I went to the psychiatrist, we talked, and he asked me a number of questions to find out if I was really inclined to cooperate with the psychoanalysis. Eventually we agreed that I would have a session each week, on a certain day, at a certain time; everything was set up. And when I asked what his fees would be and he answered me, I was automatically cured! Right then I left completely cured because I couldn't pay that much!

D: Returning to your years in secondary school, it seems as if you were heading toward a career in the church. But it's interesting that in the experience with that freethinking monk there were many different perspectives, including Marxism and psychoanalysis. Do you think these ideas had an impact on your inner struggle about a religious career?

E: Well, more than the reading of those books, I should mention the influence of my brother, Rafael, who played an important role here. He was at a military boarding school so he only came home on the weekends. At the time he was a materialist thinker and he used to constantly say things to me like:

"Well, it doesn't mean much to become a monk if you don't know anything about life—girls and parties. Because, on the contrary, if you did have that experience and you still wanted to go, well, it would mean more because you did know about other aspects of life."

He also used to pose problems to me that I now realize were very silly problems, but which caused me a lot of distress at the time. I used to go and ask the priests about them. For example, he would come tell me: "Let's see. You who are so religious, answer me this: they say that God is omnipotent . . . so with his infinite power do you think He could create a stone so large that even He couldn't lift it?"

Now of course that was a trick. If He made a stone so large He couldn't lift it, then He wouldn't be omnipotent. Another was: "Is God so powerful that He can make a round triangle?"

These were sophisms and foolishness that tormented me, and made me suffer a lot. Then I would go to the priest and say: "Listen, Father, you believe in God . . ."

And I noticed that the priest was also perplexed. And he would say: "No, you are losing your faith. Don't listen to your brother."

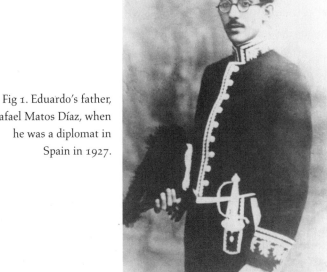

Fig 1. Eduardo's father, Rafael Matos Díaz, when he was a diplomat in Spain in 1927.

Fig 2. Eduardo's mother, Edith Moctezuma de Matos, when her husband Rafael was minister for the Dominican Republic in Panama City, 1949.

Fig 3. Eduardo at the age of two, in 1942, with his brother Rafael in Panama City.

CHAPTER TWO

The Five Breaking Points
of the Centaur

D: SO ALL THESE THINGS WERE drawing you away from religion?

E: Yes, I think that these conversations with my brother, in conjunction with my normal inclinations as a fifteen-year-old boy, beginning to take an interest in girls and all that, led me to distance myself from religion. I consider this development fundamental in my life. I began to have doubts about my religious vocation, maybe because of the influence of my brother or because of the doubts I saw in the priests. Then I began to analyze, what is God? Who is God? Does He really exist? I read books like *The Seven Storey Mountain*, by Brother Thomas Merton, in which he seeks to find God and finally ends up as a Trappist monk. I read Somerset Maugham's book *The Razor's Edge*, which is about a man who looks for God and goes everywhere and doesn't find Him and is never fulfilled. All this reading was very important to me. I was becoming more and more doubtful.

Then it was like a sort of self-psychoanalysis: at fifteen I would go walking in the night to meditate upon these questions. I lived in Las Lomas de Chapultepec. I used to go out walking alone at nine or ten at night and I would sit on a bench, I remember, on Avenida Virreyes, thinking about all these things. I had very strong doubts about the existence of God, and I would ask His forgiveness in case He existed. I felt a great deal of anguish because I was losing my faith. Until one night, very deliberately, after much analysis, I sat down and I asked for something which a Catholic should never ask for but accept on faith. I asked God for proof of His existence. I said: "Lord, You know that if You give me proof of Your existence I am going to be a saint, but if You don't give it to me tonight, I am going to give up these beliefs."

And the silence enfolded me, the night, the stars, the trees. And nothing. Perhaps I should have guessed all this was God. But I denied that possibility and said to myself: "Well, Lord, forgive me, but I don't believe in You. I have lost my faith."

The next day I felt such a relief, I felt that I was really a man, that I was no longer dependent upon superior beings, upon gods, but rather that I was a man, and that whatever I did in my infinite smallness would be my own responsibility. I felt free. The idea that remains with me from that moment is that I was alone in the universe, floating among the planets, the stars, and that the whole universe was mine, and that if I wanted to go anywhere, I would go, and if I wanted to go somewhere else I would do that too . . . and whether it was good or bad to go here or there was for me to decide. Then I felt free. For the first time I felt the liberty of being a man, a being who is master of his own destiny. I believe that the willpower I had been developing a few years earlier played a role in this.

D: What importance did this change have in later years?

E: It was a very important change in my life for this reason. It was the beginning of the awareness that I would undergo a series of profound changes or *rompimientos* in my life. Luisa (la Bruja, that's what they called my companion at the time) and I had talked about this. I now call them "the five breaking points of the Centaur." The centaur part is because she thought I was like one of those complex mythological beings. These breaking points in my life are transcendental changes, qualitative changes that combine painful

separations with uniquely new opportunities. I believe that breaking can sometimes lead to a new creation. When you have the courage and power to break with something of real value, you open the
door to create something new. So in my life every break is positive.
My first break came at fifteen years of age, with religion, as I just
mentioned. Imagine a person of that age who analyzes and dares to
take that step, to say to himself, "Enough, I no longer believe, and I
am myself, a man, and I don't depend on gods. I depend on myself
as a man." This was important, formative, and for me a creative step
into my life's pathway.

The second creative break was with the bureaucratic status and
power in my field: archaeology. The third has to do with breaking
away from the family. The fourth is the step that leads one to break
with the superfluous parts of life. The fifth and last is confronting
death. I will talk about each of them as we go along.

So this first break passed, and I began to move more and more
into materialist thinking. My reading, at fifteen years, included *The
Metamorphosis,* by Kafka, in which you identify with that person who is changed into a sort of beetle. I also read *Steppenwolf,*
by Herman Hesse. There I identified myself with the steppenwolf.
I was that solitary wolf, that distinctive individual. I entered into a
period of solitude in which my parents didn't understand me . . . I
think this is quite common in many teenagers. I began to move more
and more toward a materialist way of thinking. In those years, when
I was in preparatory school, in high school with my friends, I had
my first sexual experiences at fifteen years of age. A new world was
appearing, I kept discovering new things. I still felt a strong spirituality and there were times when I meditated a lot in the afternoons.
When I was fifteen and broke away from religion and began to go to
parties, my friends were older than I was, twenty, twenty-one years
old. Some were already studying architecture and working. Others,
like my cousin Mauro, were pilots. I really admired my cousin and

my friends. They called me "the priest" because of my wanting to become a La Salle Brother. But I idolized them; if there was a fight at one of the parties, they were the ones who defended me. I had a great admiration for them. For example, we would go to the brothels every weekend. I felt like the painter Toulouse Lautrec who lived in a brothel. We would go on Saturday nights and the girls already knew me by name. I didn't go to bed with them because I had no money, but we talked very amiably and played twenty-cent poker until some client showed up. My friends did go up to their rooms with them because they had money to pay them. (From the saints to the "saints.") I remember there is a Mexican novel called *Santa* by Federico Gamboa that's about a prostitute. For me, these were impressive experiences, fantastic, because then when I was back in school with boys of my own age, who were very innocent kids, I would mention: "Listen, last night I was with these whores. . . ."

And they wouldn't believe me.

So there were maybe two or three years when I was going to these parties, hanging around the prostitutes, and these adventures expanded my knowledge of human life. One has one's idols. My cousin, Frank Álvarez, was very strong; I admired him. Later, when I was in preparatory school, I had my first girlfriend, named Susana. To be sure, I took a long time to "declare myself," as we say in Mexico, to tell her I wanted her to be my girlfriend. It was at a kermess, a party at Cristóbal Colón School when I finally made up my mind and told her: "Susana, I have something very important to say to you, but look, first let's go over and see this game . . ."

I couldn't get up the nerve to tell her, but finally I did, and she said "yes." I only saw her once afterward. After that there were others . . . anyway, we'll talk about that later.

D: What was happening then with your studies?

E: At that time I entered the School of Anthropology. This was in 1959. In the school's courses we had to take physical anthropology, the evolution of man, the Neanderthal, the Australopithecus, and others. My interest in the materialist approach to social history became stronger. I remember being assigned the book *Our Primitive Contemporaries* by George Murdock, about various tribes, where ancient customs, economies, social organization, and religions were described. I read about the Semang, the Arunta, the Huitotos in Colombia, in short, about various ancient peoples and their indigenous ways of thinking. I was attracted to this kind of study.

D: Who taught the class?

E: That class was taught by Calixta Guiteras, a Cuban ethnologist. She was an excellent teacher. At that time, in 1959, Castro was in the Sierra Maestra fighting against Batista; he would win during that year. I remember that we students wholeheartedly supported Fidel. Our Cuban teacher was also pro-Fidel, so that had quite an impact on me. I started to join progressive organizations and liberation movements. I began to sense an inner transformation the more I got into it and read the *Communist Manifesto* and the writings of Stalin, although I didn't understand much; I felt that my spirituality was being lost and that the loss was a negative. I felt that something very deep within me, something very good, was being lost. But I was involved in the revolutionary struggle . . . I tended to ignore this awareness. But there was always a small spiritual strand that reminded me and told me "Wait, now, yes, it's alright, you're becoming political, but there is something deep within you, an internal energy that calls you toward reflective afternoons, toward moments of melancholy and solitude."

To sum up that whole period, I would say that from the age of fourteen or fifteen to eighteen was a very important time, in which

I first broke away from religion, and I began to think, to speculate a lot, and to come alive intellectually in a new way. A period when at times I would be watching the sunset and thinking about these questions and there would be a moment of such emotion that one feels as if one is vibrating inside. And I began to gradually lose the intensity of these feelings with my entering into materialism. I felt it very strongly as a loss, but as I said, I had to be involved in the social struggle.

The interior cabin

D: It seems that as your feelings of God waned, you felt a kind of liberation. Yet this liberation was difficult and complex. It reminds me of the title of a book about my teacher Mircea Eliade titled *Ordeal by Labyrinth*. Do you see these years and changes as a series of ordeals?

E: Well, I remember that when my friends and I went to parties I would ask a girl to dance, and then there were always the typical questions: "What is your name?" "What school do you go to?" and usually everyone followed that with "Have you been to the movies lately?" "What movies have you seen?" . . . but not me. I would immediately ask her: "And you, what do you believe would make you happy?"

The poor girl would just look at me, not answer at all or say almost anything and I would begin to explain to her what happiness meant to me. I always said it would be to be alone in a cabin in some place with pines, a forest, with a distant landscape with my fireplace and my pipe. I smoked a pipe from an early age. Even when I was in secondary school at thirteen or fourteen years old I went around with a pencil in my mouth, or with a hollow twig shaped like a pipe. One day my mother asked me: "Listen, what is that you've got there?"

And I answered: "It's a pipe."

She looked surprised and asked me: "Do you want a pipe?"

"Yes."

"Well, come on, we'll buy you one."

And we went out and she bought me a pipe and tobacco. She told me, "Smoke it." So I went to school smoking my pipe and with written permission signed by my mother that I was allowed to smoke. So then of course I got the attention of the teachers and the envy of my friends. "Matos's parents gave him permission to smoke!" But let's get back to that cabin with a fireplace, with the pipe. That image was present in me for a long time. And that image of happiness was what I told the girls about. They stood looking at me as if to say, "This guy is crazy" and yet it was something very important to me, because it was a way of thinking. Much later when I was studying anthropology, I had this friend, Victoria Uribe, who was a Colombian. I told her about the image and her response was: But you don't have to go away to a real cabin to have that cabin. You can have an interior cabin.

This really stayed with me. More recently, when I read the book by Mircea Eliade about the test of the labyrinth, I saw that at one point in it, he says that the thought of Krishna, what Krishna teaches, is precisely that you don't have to go to a place of meditation, or to a field, a forest or a monastery, but that you can do it internally. It is an experience, an interior thing. So I believe this was also very important because this idea took root deeply in me, along with another which was to analyze myself and see how I would characterize myself. I felt that I was a melancholy person who liked the evening better than the morning, the autumn better than the spring, the color gray better than yellow, a rainy day better than a clear day, that is, those gray hues of the rain, melancholy, in short all those elements. And I arrived at this conclusion: one common denominator of sensitive people was precisely this . . . solitude, silence, evening, autumn.

In that period I wrote some poems, but now I would call them meditations, on this presence of the gray and the autumn. There is a place in one of these meditations where I say, "I know you are there but I cannot see you." That is, I was involved in an interior search that was crucial to me, but that I couldn't manage to express concretely.

D: It is interesting that you mentioned Mircea Eliade because Mircea also always smoked a pipe. There are a lot of photographs where he appears with a pipe. He had a lot of pipes and was often smoking. Some people know that smoking is a restful thing. But it also symbolizes Eliade's interest in the use of fire, heat, and the practices of shamanism. Curiously, you also smoke a pipe.

E: Really, I always enjoyed it so much that, at times when I didn't have a girlfriend or I broke up with a girl, I would say that I had my companion which was my pipe and I would smoke it. Always, from then to the present day, my pipe has always accompanied me. It is a part of me. When I wrote a poem called "My Testament" dedicated to my daughter, Daniela, at one point I mentioned my pipe as a vital part of my life.

D: Do you have a favorite tobacco? For Eliade, for example, the best was Tres Estrellas.

E: Yes. I usually smoke a blend called North Sea, which is pretty tasty, and has a nice aroma like the bouquet of a woman.

Fig 4. Eduardo as a student in Preparatoria, 1958.

Fig 5. Eduardo at seventeen years of age practicing his skill with a bull, 1958.

CHAPTER THREE

From Religion to Anthropology

THE NATIONAL SCHOOL OF ANTHROPOLOGY AND HISTORY

D: YOU HAVE TALKED ABOUT YOUR INTEREST in anthropology. What was it that attracted you to anthropology instead of theology or other sciences?

E: In high school I was very undecided about what I was going to study. My brother was attending classes at the School of Architecture. At the time architecture was somewhat attractive to me. But mathematics terrified me, anything to do with physics and chemistry was awful for me . . . I always failed. In 1957 I was in my first year of high school and I had no clear idea what to do. I was in the Cristóbal Colón preparatory school, which is a La Salle school. Fortunately, one day a friend, Luis Vargas, who later graduated as a medical doctor, and eventually as an anthropologist, and presently combines the two disciplines, loaned me a book which proved decisive for me. It was the one by C. W. Ceram entitled *Gods, Graves and Scholars*. I read that book . . . look what a significant title! *Gods, Graves and Scholars.* . . . There are three levels: the celestial level, the terrestrial level, and the underworld. The part that enchanted me was the part about Egypt: how they kept finding the pharaohs, all the stories about what had happened. I was thrilled to read how Howard Carter discovered the tomb of Tutankhamun. That book was the key to my becoming impassioned about archaeology. It also caused some anxiety, as I asked, "Well, and where am I going to study archaeology? Will I have to go out of the country?" And once again it was Luis who helped me, because when I told him I wanted to study archaeology, he told me: "Well, yes, there is a school here in Mexico where you can study archaeology."

"What?"—I answered—"There is a school?"

"Well, of course. Dr. Davalos is the director of the Instituto Nacional de Antropología e Historia [INAH], and you could go to the Escuela Nacional de Antropología e Historia [ENAH]."

I went to the school immediately and asked for the brochures, to see what was involved in that career, and I enrolled to study archaeology.

D: Before that moment, had you ever visited any archaeological ruins in Mexico?

E: No, not at all. I was very ignorant about Mexican archaeology, and instead had paid attention to Egyptian things. So then I told my parents about my plans. It seemed fine to my father, at least he never said anything. My mother was worried and told me: "Listen, son, it's all right. If you want to study that, study it. But . . . wouldn't it be good to take some classes in the School of Business and Banking? Because I don't think archaeologists earn much."

Obviously, she was worried about my economic future. So, although she didn't forbid it, she tried to dissuade me so that I would study something that guaranteed a good living standard. I answered: "No, mama. There is no way I am going to get into banking."

Once again it was Luis who cleared the way for me. When I told him about my mother's point of view, he told me: "You may well die of hunger, but you'll die very happy that you studied what you wanted . . ."

I enrolled and began my studies. At that time, it was a four-year program. This was in 1959. That's how I began my time as a university student.

From Rilke to the revolution

D: You have mentioned your interest in revolutionary movements. You even experienced a revolutionary event when you were a child and the embassy that served as your home was attacked. Later you developed an interest in archaeology, in the past. How were these two aspects of social revolution and exploring the past combined during your anthropological education?

E: Well, it was interesting, because ENAH had always been characterized as a leftist school. So I was in my element, as we say in Mexico, *en mi mero mole*. That is, I was studying the past, which I liked, and I was also participating actively in demonstrations and all that. But, that subtle tenuous thread, that interior part of me that was still alive, that thing which I can't really name—maybe spirituality—survived and sometimes whispered to me, "Wait, you are no longer vibrant . . . what's going on?" At that time I had a girlfriend who was studying in the school with me; she enrolled in the same year as I did. Her name was Rosalinda Monzón. She was a very pretty girl, had a rather Egyptian-looking face, and she was very important in my life, not so much because she was my girlfriend, but because she gave me another very important key: she gave me the book *Letters to a Young Poet* by Rainer Maria Rilke. When I read that book my ruminations about the spell of evening, solitude, silence, in short my introspective life, came alive in a new way through the writings of the poet Rilke. I identified with him immediately. That book was fundamental to my future life and thought. It is ten letters in which he answers a young poet, a certain Kappus, and speaks to him about love, solitude, and art. In short, there is a complete philosophy, a complete way of thought behind what Rilke is expressing. From that moment I became an avid student of Rilke. This helped to nurture and maintain my introspective life.

I combined these readings and internal reflections with demon-strations, the struggle, exercises with other students. I walked, par-ticipated in student movements, handed out flyers. We supported Fidel Castro's Cuba. I still believe that the Cuban Revolution was the first great, truly anti-imperialist revolution. And I believe it was the revolution of the youth of that time, the early seventies. It was our revolution. Che Guevara, Fidel Castro, Raúl, Camilo, they were all our guidelines inside the revolutionary movement. I'm going to tell you about something that took place when the United States backed the invasion of Cuba at the Bay of Pigs. We held a meeting, in anger, at the School of Economics in the Universidad Nacional Autónoma de Mexico (UNAM). There were leaders speaking: "Comrades! We must support Cuba! The imperialists have invaded. . . !"

And everyone there answered in chorus: "Fidel! Fidel! Give the Yankees Hell!"

Suddenly, some guys started handing out sheets of paper to the demonstrators, saying: "It's for everybody to fill out who wants to go fight against Imperialism in Cuba."

We all wanted to sign up. I took the sheet and started to fill it out: Name: Eduardo Matos Moctezuma. Address: Telephone: Do you know how to use firearms? Yes! In Cuba, what weapons would you like to use? We all named the most difficult: tanks, bazookas . . . We filled out the questionnaires and they gathered them up. The meeting went on, and this guy jumped up on the stage, grabbed the micro-phone and said: "Comrades! Be careful! How many filled out the papers they were handing out?"

The answer was unanimous: "Everyone! Everyone!"

"Don't be idiots! The guys who handed those out were from the government! Now they have all of your names and addresses."

As you can see, we were still very innocent . . . But at the same time, I also had the other aspect, the guideline of Rilke, the experience of solitude, of profound thought. And also, my learning, the process of preparing myself to search for the past. So there were three elements which combined in a certain way. At times the revolutionary would come to the fore, at others the sensitive man who lived every evening profoundly would flourish inside me, as well as my thirst for archaeology. Each of them helped to determine my life.

D. It is interesting that in this period of integration, there is a woman. A woman from another world who is opening something in you, and that you respond in that way. It appears that women play a major role in your growth.

E: Of course. I was always very inclined to fall in love, and I had a lot of luck. If there was a girl I liked, I was always lucky enough to have her take me seriously. I mean, I never suffered the frustration of being rejected. I think that is also pretty important. And women have played very important roles throughout my life. At that time I mostly ran around with girls from ENAH. Some of them were my girlfriends. I also met a lot of girls I liked and found attractive outside school. For example, Rosalinda, who more than anything else gave me the key to open another pathway. The years passed and she left the school, a very intelligent girl. She married and had children. She died a few years ago. But I always remember her with a lot of tenderness, precisely because of that key she gave me that allowed me to enter the world of Rilke, and therefore to reinforce my internal world.

D: Can you tell us more about the political climate in Mexico during those times? For example, what was the political event that had the most impact on the students at ENAH? You have talked about the Cuban Revolution, but what was happening inside Mexico at that time? What people or events, what demonstrations stand out in your memory?

E: While I was a student, fundamentally the common denominator was the Cuban Revolution. It was more an external aspect that was occasionally manifested in opposition to the government, because of the attitudes of the government. I remember that in those days I belonged to an organization called the Latin American Movement which was a movement in support of Cuba. We were there with some friends whom I really loved, with Teresa and Carmen Losada, for example. They were daughters of Spaniards who had come to Mexico because of their Civil War. And of course now that I mention the Spanish Civil War, I've always had a great fondness for learning about it. I've never known why, but I was entranced by reading about that war. Of course, I was always inclined toward the Republican side and against Franco. My conversations with these friends and with other children of Spaniards were very important to me. I always thought it was a terrible defeat for the Spanish people and for avant-garde thought. Poets like León Felipe, Alberti, and García Lorca were important to me there. Some of my anthropology professors like Pedro Bosch Gimpera, Juan Comas, and José Luis Lorenzo came from that Spain. We saw and lived with that defeated Spain, though I would say only temporarily defeated. I loved to hear the songs of the Fifth Regiment, all those songs we also sang, and, well, we felt as though we were becoming true revolutionaries without having fired a shot.

In Mexico we had the government of López Mateos, with Mr. Jaime Torres Bodet, who was a great intellectual and poet, as secretary of education. But after the next election, we had the government of Gustavo Díaz Ordaz which was really unfortunate. At that time I was a schoolteacher, having graduated in 1965. The year 1968 was a very tense time because the student movement had begun and was growing stronger in Mexico and around the world. The student movement had begun in France and Germany and it all seemed to peak in May 1968. All those European student leaders like Cohn-Bendit, nicknamed

"Dani The Red," and all those people . . . and there was the Vietnam War and the antiwar movement in the American universities.

D: And in the United States the African Americans were demonstrating also, with Martin Luther King.

E: Exactly. That's when that was happening and we heard about Black Power. So there was a lot of commotion and in Mexico the government of Díaz Ordaz took power. The movement of student strikes was repressed; the military went to the Preparatory School and blew the door open with a bazooka, and the soldiers went in. The people were demonstrating, all the universities were against the government; it was really a strong movement, with impressive, massive demonstrations.

D: And this happened during the Olympic Games?

E: Yes, a little before, the same year. Demonstrations of four hundred thousand people completely filled the Zócalo. Then there was a very noble step taken by Octavio Paz. Octavio was then the ambassador to India and he resigned his post. He sent a letter stating that he was not in agreement with the actions the government was taking and he resigned his post. For us this was an example, a decision that he took, a very noble act. Finally the movement was crushed in an extremely violent way, brutally, on October 2, 1968, in Tlatelolco. There was a great massacre of students. The students and the professors who supported the movement had gathered at 6:00 p.m. in the Plaza of Three Cultures. By mere coincidence, I was not there. I had planned to go, but something came up, I don't even remember what, but anyway, I couldn't go. And that night, at about 8:30, I was near ENAH and I ran into a fellow student from the school. She was very shaken, and she asked me, "Eduardo, were you at Tlatelolco?"

"No. Why?"

"It was horrible. They killed students. The soldiers aimed to kill."

The next day we learned the details of the massacre. This is something that has remained with all of us, with a lot of people; many intellectuals like Elena Poniatowska have come out against that massacre by the government. We lived this up close; we could touch it, see it, and feel it very profoundly.

D: This was a time of great change. You had the Cuban Revolution, and also the memories of people from Spain, and inside Mexico itself there was profound unrest and suffering.

E: Exactly. I described that period more or less this way: I said, damn, what a historical coincidence! You had this unrest in the United States, in all of Europe—France, Germany, and in Mexico. And there were the governments of three fundamental leaders. In the Soviet Union you had Nikita Kruschev, whom I always considered a simple, likeable, and intelligent man, who came from a working-class family. He began the movement against Stalin. There was a certain opening up in the Soviet Union. But coincidentally at the same time you had Kennedy in the United States. And, like Kruschev, who realized the Soviet Union could be criticized, Kennedy also saw that the United States could be criticized and should be changed. I believe that his position in favor of change later brought about his assassination, his death. And in the Vatican, there was John XXIII, the Pope who also brought change into the church by means of an internal critique. So, these political factors are really interesting because a general process of change turned the seventies into a crucial decade of the twentieth century.

Since the future is uncertain, let us turn to the past

D: Did all of this have an impact on Mexican anthropology, on archaeology, on the thinking of the students in their search for the past?

E: Yes, it's an interesting story. I used to say, somewhat jokingly, "Since the future is uncertain, let's turn to the past." And then, of course, came all my experiences in my career, all my training in the field. My training came fundamentally with Professor José Luis Lorenzo in Tehuacán, Puebla, and Tepeapulco, Hidalgo, which is a site where I have always liked working. Even so, one of the first sites where I excavated, around 1961, was in Tlatelolco under Paco González Rul, as part of my work in INAH, which I had recently joined. Later, while I was working in collaboration with Carlos Navarrete in Malpaso, Chiapas, I had some fascinating experiences. It was in 1966 and they were building a dam in Malpaso. So the town they had created there was an artificial town of five thousand workers, a few engineers, and twenty-five women, twenty-four of whom were prostitutes. The other woman was the owner of a pharmacy who was a friend of ours and used to sell us some things on credit. It wasn't just a pharmacy, she had some of everything. Some interesting things happened there. One day Navarrete had to go back to Mexico City and left me in charge of the project. We had two teams working there: the team from INAH and the team from the New World Archaeological Foundation, who were Mormons. We lived in the archaeological sites. I was the only one who was in the village, because that was our connection with the engineers and the funding. One day I went to the Post Office, which of course was a shed, an improvised structure, to pick up the mail. There was a fat guy inside who was referred to as the "director of the post office." So this fat guy says to me, "Listen, Professor. Do you all have any enemies?"

The question seemed very strange to me:

"Good heavens! No, I don't think we have any enemies."

"Well, that's really odd, because we had a burglary Saturday night here in the Post Office, and the only letters that were opened were the letters that came for you, for the archaeologists!"

I answered: "But the only honest people around here are the archaeologists, the engineers, and a few of the workers . . ."

I should clarify that among the workers there were some very fine people, but there were also those who had killed someone and fled and joined up to work for us so they wouldn't be found. We had a worker, for example, who was called "el Diablo" who had killed several people. Anyway, there is something I haven't mentioned to you, which is that at the time I was a stutterer. So I said to the fat guy: "L-l-listen, b-but tell me wh- what happened."

"Well, I am going to file a report because we think some of you must be the guilty parties who stole the mail."

I was worried. I went back, and when Navarrete returned I told him the whole story: "I'm worried. This guy is going to accuse us archaeologists of burglary. . . ."

"Let me go talk to him"—he answered.

When he came back, Carlos was dying of laughter: "Listen. He thinks you. . . ."

"What?"

"The fat guy says you are the guilty party."

"What, me?"

"Yeah, and he's going to bring in the law."

"But why?"

"Because he says when he started telling you about the burglary, you got real nervous and started stuttering."

And I said: "Oh man! If that's his evidence, he's already lost. Because I'm a bigger stutterer than Demosthenes."

D: Eduardo, you have mentioned that you were a stutterer. Was that true throughout your youth? How did that change during your life?

E: Yes. I stuttered from childhood. I imagine that it was a manifestation of insecurity. But I also believe that practice of mine of the sacrifices, which made me develop an iron will, must have helped me to cure myself. One day, when I was already a professional, already graduated, I said to myself, "I can't go on being a stutterer, I have to give lectures and classes, I have to engage in academic activities. This can't continue, it's not possible." So then, I decided that I would no longer stutter, and I began, like Demosthenes, who placed pebbles under his tongue, to learn to speak. I didn't use that method, but I began to speak. I remember that was when we were working in Teotihuacan, around 1963. We were in the Palace of the Butterflies, excavating. It was my job to excavate the Palace of the Plumed Snails. Jorge Acosta, a person whom I admire greatly, was directing the excavation of that sector. Then later they gave me Zone 9 in the Street of the Dead, which was my responsibility, and on which I published a small report in the *Anales de Antropología* of UNAM. But at that time we used to travel to Teotihuacan in a bus that picked us up at 7:00 in the morning, and I used to act up quite a bit. The whole team of archaeologists and restorers was there, and because of the early hour they were about half asleep. I would start singing opera, just to bug them. One thing I used to do was to suddenly announce, "OK, I'm going to give you a political speech: Gentlemen! Comrades!...." And I would start talking, and without stuttering the whole time. When I finished, if they asked me something I would stutter again. I remember one occasion that was very painful for me because I had to give a lecture, and I told Ricardo Ferrer, who had invited me to present it, "Ricardo, I'm really scared, because I'm a stutterer . . ."

And he said: "Well, let's see how you do."

I was suffering tremendously because the moment when I would have to participate was getting closer. Fortunately, the last lecturer before me ran very long, so I was spared the ordeal for that day. I left without giving the lecture. But something that was very helpful to me, was that Miguel Messmacher, another person I admire greatly, an architect and archaeologist, very intelligent, invited me to be his aide in his class "Arquitectura Prehispánica." That was in 1967. So I presented the class stuttering, but I kept getting a little better. Teaching the class, meeting with the students, I had to talk all the time. And there came a time during those years when I conquered the problem and was no longer a stutterer. Now it's the opposite; you can't stop me talking. I give about thirty lectures a year, I teach classes and there's no problem. But I do believe my willpower overcame the stuttering problem.

The teachers: from Marquina to Bernal

L: Tell me about your teachers.

E: Well, I remember that when I entered ENAH one of the professors who impressed me for various reasons was José Luis Lorenzo. He taught the course "Arqueología General," and everyone was afraid of him, because he was very strict. At the beginning of the course he asked, "Let's see. How many of you speak English? Raise your hands."

Two or three students raised their hands.

"How many understand French?"

A girl raised a delicate hand. He stood looking at us with a thunderous stare and skewered us:

"Students, I don't think you are going to pass this course because the basic reading here is in English, primarily, and also in other languages."

When I heard those words I gave myself up for dead. The course started, and at the end, we waited for our grades. I was thinking that if I failed I could ask for a transfer into a Physical Anthropology program. But, as it turned out, I was elated to learn that I had received a 6. They said that a 6 in Lorenzo's class was like an 8 from any other professor.

Even so, with Lorenzo we learned to have a different understanding of archaeology. Through him we learned about Gordon Childe, with whom I identified immediately because of his materialist and social approach to the discipline. Other important professors in my development were Johanna Faulhaber, who taught our class in Physical Anthropology based on a book by Dr. Juan Comas: *Manual de Antropología Física*. I also had linguistics with Moisés Romero. There were a number of professors who taught me a lot. Among them I remember Wigberto Jiménez Moreno with his course, "Historia Antigua de México." Also there was Professor Barbro Dahlgren, who was a little scattered but knew a lot about ethnography. Of course Román Piña Chan, with whom I entered the labyrinths of Mesoamerica.

D: How was Piña Chan important in your education?

E: In 1960 he published his book *Mesoamérica*, which presented a social view of archaeology. This interested me greatly, and I always said that Piña Chan represented a sociological current within archaeology. In my opinion, Piña is one of the archaeologists who knew most about Mesoamerica. He had a great understanding of ceramics, the stages and their chronology. He had worked in such sites as Tlatilco and other preclassical sites. Besides, unlike Lorenzo, he was generous with his students.

Another teacher I remember fondly is Mr. Pedro Bosch Gimpera. He was very much a gentleman. He always had a large cigar in his mouth and carried a large satchel of maps that he would put up on the walls of the classroom. He taught the course called "Prehistoria y Protohistoria." He talked to us about the Franco-Cantabrian region and the campaniform vase. When I graduated he chaired my committee. Another personality was Mr. Pablo Martínez del Río, the director of the school, always elegantly dressed in his vest, bowler hat and even spats! I didn't happen to have a class with Ignacio Marquina, who taught pre-hispanic architecture. I took that course from Miguel Messmacher, with whom I worked later on various projects.

L: You have mentioned a number of professors. I remember that Eliade, on one of his visits to Mexico, met Jiménez Moreno. That had an impact on him, so much so that he wrote in one of his journals, "Jiménez Moreno knows everything; what a shame I didn't have an opportunity to study with him." Could you tell us more about the contribution made to Mexican archaeologists by such professors as Jiménez Moreno?

E: Wigberto was an autodidact and during the decades from the fifties to the seventies he shaped several generations with his course, "The Ancient History of Mexico." He looked like a priest. His clothing was always very proper and always black.

He was from the state of Guanajuato, as was Antonio Pompa, the director of the library, who always joked with Wigberto. Don Güi Güi, as he was called among the students, was an old-fashioned historian, one of those who especially study the succession of rulers, their lineages, but he also had a profound knowledge of historical sources. He presented almost none of the sociological questions, for which he was already being criticized by certain historians. His position was made clear in his books. One of the last images I have of this professor is when he directed ENAH and he was called on to confront problems related to the student situation. Finally he left the post which devolved upon another historian, Carlos Martínez Marín, whom I succeeded as director of the ENAH in 1971. One detail about Don Wigberto: he never wore a watch. He used to say that time was irrelevant; that he didn't care if his discourse went much longer than the forty-five minutes allotted to him.

Myself, I am marvelously, strictly punctual.

L: You always arrive early?

E: It is a hair-raising obsession.

L: Tell us more about Miguel Messmacher whom you mentioned. What was his contribution to your studies?

E: Miguel was an architect and archaeologist. He had presented his thesis on prehistory at ENAH. He was a brilliant man and there was an immediate empathy between him and me. Around 1966 he was given the responsibility of the work that was going on at Cholula, Puebla. He immediately called on me to oversee the fieldwork.

I should clarify here that there were two parts of this work The first was directed by Messmacher with his own integral and interdisciplinary approach. This involved the participation of other specialists like the linguist Daniel Cazés, social anthropologists like Margarita Nolasco and Mercedes Olivera, and many others, including architects and veterinarians. We were trying to revalidate the idea of integrated projects applied to a defined region, as had been done by Manuel Gamio in Teotihuacan between 1917 and 1920, but using the advances which modern anthropological science had achieved by then.

Ignacio Marquina was to direct the second part with the support of old guard archaeologists like Jorge Acosta, Ponciano Salazar, and Florencia Müller. What happened was that the dominant approach in archaeology, then in the hands of Alfonso Caso, didn't agree with the approach we had taken for the project. They said that this was not archaeology. A commission was formed, headed by Caso, which decided to terminate the Cholula Project. In reality, this involved a generational struggle between a traditional vision of anthropology, represented by Alfonso Caso, and a more modern position like that directed by Miguel Messmacher.

Messmacher was important because he was an intelligent person with whom one could talk and discuss anthropological questions. He had read widely and was accessible. For that reason I have always been sorry he withdrew from anthropology to dedicate himself to other things because I think he could have been a really eminent anthropologist.

L: To continue the subject of your teachers, your supervisors, the people who influenced you, tell us about Marquina, Acosta, and Bernal.

E: I'd have to start with Don Jorge Acosta. He was educated in England and was a friend of Eric Thompson, who was a specialist on the Maya. In fact, his early work was done in Belize along with Thompson. My first contact with Acosta was in Teotihuacan around 1962, when the Teotihuacan Project was being directed by Ignacio Bernal. I was to act as field assistant to Don Jorge in the Palace of the Butterflies. It turned out that he was named to head the Department of Pre-hispanic Monuments. This meant that he had to be in Mexico City at least two or three times a week, which left me in charge of the excavations. I got to excavate part of the Palace of the Butterflies and all of the Palace of the Plumed Snails. The northern part was almost intact, with impressions of the places where the lintels of the doors had rested. We even found some remains of the wood they were made of. But the southern part was very deteriorated and was reconstructed by Don Jorge. I want to point out that even then I was not in favor of reconstruction, by which I mean adding missing parts to a building. I think one should respect the evidence exactly as it appears in the process of excavation and preserve it carefully. Don Jorge was a prominent reconstructor. Nevertheless, I have to acknowledge that watching the handling of the construction materials was important for me, because on the Templo Mayor Project I was able to apply these techniques not in reconstruction, but certainly in the preservation of the original stairways.

And then we have the architect Ignacio Marquina. I feel an enormous admiration for him. I got to know him through his publications, especially one which I consider to be a classic of Mexican archaeology: *Arquitectura prehispánica,* and another which proved to be very helpful in the Templo Mayor Project, *El Templo Mayor de México.* In 1967 he was chosen to head the Department of Pre-hispanic Monuments, after the Cholula Project was dissolved. He was to have headed the second part of it. Since I was no longer involved after Messmacher left, I was named associate director of Pre-hispanic Monuments. So I became close to the architect Marquina.

L: What year would that be?

E: That would be the end of 1967 and early 1968. I came to know Marquina as a true gentleman; for one thing, like myself, he was very punctual. He would always arrive at the same time and slowly climb the stairs of INAH at Córdoba 45, until he reached the offices of the director of Pre-hispanic Monuments on the third floor. I got along with him immediately. He was an honest, straightforward man, graceful in every way: in his way of speaking, in his manner of dress, and in his actions. I remember once when there was some trouble between archaeologists in the department and he told me: "Look, Matos"—He never called me Eduardo—"call these two gentlemen in so we can get to the bottom of this difficulty between them."

When they were together, Don Ignacio was very direct: "Sir, you have said one thing or another and so-and-so is not in agreement. I want this business settled here and now."

The embarrassment of these colleagues when directly confronted helped to avoid further gossip. One particular case the architect handled this way was when the physical anthropologist Roberto Jiménez

Ovando came to see Marquina to inform him that in the excavations at Cuicuilco, which were being carried out in preparation for the upcoming Olympic Games, the archaeologist Roberto Gallegos had made a gift of a small collection of ceramics excavated there to the architect Pedro Ramírez Vázquez. He immediately called Gallegos in; the four of us were in the office and without mincing words Marquina called Gallegos on it. And an argument began between Gallegos and Jiménez Ovando. Marquina didn't allow any gossip and tried to clear up these situations immediately and directly.

In his free time the architect was writing his *Memorias* with a broad-pointed pen. He didn't dictate or type, but wrote by hand. I learned a lot from him about how to deal with people, and about honor and integrity. I remember that because of the death of Dr. Eusebio Dávalos Hurtado, the director of INAH in 1968, they named Dr. Ignacio Bernal as director. He had been the director of the National Museum of Anthropology. Marquina called me in and told me: "Look, Matos, I have my resignation here to present to the new director, I wanted to let you know in case of anything that might happen. I also want to ask you a question: tell me, Matos, if you had to name the director of the Museum of Anthropology, which of the archaeologists would you choose?"

I was perplexed. I immediately thought of who might be named, thought of some with strengths and with weaknesses. I mentioned some names with certain reservations. Finally he said: "Really, Matos, is there nobody who could take charge of the Museum?"

"Well, from our discussion, it seems not, because the Museum is very important."

"It's sad to arrive at that conclusion. I mentioned it to you because Dr. Bernal asked me who would be good to place there and I couldn't recommend anyone. That's why I wanted to hear the opinion of a young man, to see if he could shed any light on the question, but in fact, there isn't anyone, right?"

The case of Ignacio Bernal is different. I even came to criticize him for his approach to archaeology, since I thought he was an idealist. I have later gone back and reread his works and some have had an impact on me. For example, I think the first chapter of his *Historia de la arqueología en México* is really excellent. If I someday wanted to make an anthology of archaeological thought, I might well include this piece of Bernal's writing. Also, at that time nobody thought to suggest that Teotihuacan was militaristic, it was considered a theocratic society, and that's what we were taught. Don Ignacio introduced the idea that it might have been a militaristic empire.

It was pleasant to talk to Ignacio Bernal since he was a very cultured man, and this was interesting because in our field there are archaeologists who are very capable within their branch of knowledge, but who can't be drawn out of it, you can't talk to them about art or literature. I was with him a time or two at his house in his splendid library and we talked about a lot of subjects not necessarily associated with archaeology.

L: Do you have any stories about these visits to Dr. Bernal's house?

E: On one occasion when the noted French archaeologist Jacques Soustelle came to Mexico, Don Ignacio gave a dinner. I should clarify that in the field of anthropology Bernal was considered a thorough elitist; not just anyone was invited to his house. He was very selective and kept his distance. There were eight or ten of us at the dinner: Dr. Soustelle, who was the guest of honor; Dr. Bernal and his wife, who were the hosts; Dr. Jiménez Moreno; others whom I can't recall; and myself. I was a little nervous being in the presence of personalities like Jacques Soustelle—whose books I had read, and with whom I later had a good friendship—and my professor Jiménez. After a magnificent meal, we moved into the library to have coffee and a

fine cognac. We were standing there when I started to light a ciga-
rette, but I dropped my matches. When I bent over to pick them
up, I bumped my butt into a beautiful silver candelabra that held
a white candle. The whole thing went down! Imagine my fright!
The candle broke into three pieces. The candelabra was not damaged but I was immensely embarrassed. Don Ignacio came over to
me very calmly and asked in his usual deliberate voice, "What happened, Eduardo?"

He called me by my name, while I never addressed him as other
than Doctor, as was fitting. With great trepidation I was just able to
answer: "Well, here. . . ."

"Don't worry about it. It's a broken candle . . ."

And with that simplicity, he helped me to recover my composure.
I sat for a while, drank one cognac, which was followed by others, and
had no more trouble.

L: Did your love for the history of archaeology come from your reading of Bernal? How did you get interested in the subject?

E: It was precisely the reading of two articles on the subject by Don
Ignacio that aroused my interest. I loved them and began to learn
more. I turned to him as director of my thesis for the doctorate in
anthropology at UNAM when he was the director of the Museum
of Anthropology. I can't be certain, but I think in a way I motivated
him to write his *Historia de la arqueología en México*, since that was
exactly the subject of my thesis. I took him a scheme for division into
chapters and a bibliography and told him: "Doctor Bernal, I have read
your articles and they have influenced me greatly, I am fascinated
by the subject and I would like you to be the director of my doctoral
thesis. I'm bringing you this scheme for division into chapters, and
asking to begin working with you."

"Well, of course, of course! How interesting."

I imagine he must have thought "Man, a subject I have been working on, and here this youngster comes proposing it. I had better finish quickly, and then this kid can write whatever he likes . . ." In 1979 he published his *Historia de la arqueología en México*, which has been very important to me.

Pedro Armillas and Mircea Eliade

D: The first contact I had with your work was through Pedro Armillas, one of my great professors at the University of Illinois. I remember well that I was in the process of writing my doctoral dissertation about Quetzalcóatl when I found out about Pedro Armillas. I called him and told him that I had read about him in books by Eric Wolf and others, and we agreed to meet. The first time I saw him I was impressed by his voice, his pronounced limp, and his stature, and we eventually became friends. Pedro did me the favor of giving lectures in the Chicano barrio of Pilsen. Later when I wanted to do research in Mexico, he offered to write me a letter of introduction. He wrote you a letter asking you to give me permission to visit archaeological centers associated with Quetzalcóatl. Pedro Armillas must have been one of your professors. How did you meet him, and what memories do you have of his influence on you and his impact on your studies of Mesoamerica?

E: Armillas meant and still means a lot to me for several reasons. First, I see my passion for the Spanish Civil War in the context of Pedro Armillas, a man damaged by the war, that limp he had caused by an enemy mortar; his Spanish vigor, his robust figure. He sometimes seemed to me like a helmeted conquistador. So then, on the one hand, I was very attracted by him as a personality, but even more so from the point of view of academics, because I had read some of Pedro's writing and articles in school. Pedro was not one to write great big books, but rather articles with a lot of content. I remember some of them, for example when he talks about social and economic systems, and the materialist position he held. I also remember an article he wrote in the fifties, in which he proposed an evolutionary process in Mesoamerica.

I think Pedro was right in proposing that process. Later we got all this business of the "Classical" and "Postclassical" which I have always been against. When I read Pedro I can see that he takes the economic element to be fundamental, and talks in terms of agricultural and proto-agricultural. Besides that, he conceives of Mesoamerica from the end of the so-called "Preclassical" until the time of the conquest as a unity, which is what I have been arguing also. So, in contrast to the idealistic position, I see Pedro as a symbol of a struggle like that of the Spanish Civil War, but also as a symbol of a materialist approach that's very important within academia, in its conception of history. I would say that his influence was definitive in the conception I have of the process of development in Mesoamerica. I believe Pedro was right and I identify myself with him in the way he understood this process.

I remember the day I met Pedro Armillas. It was in the INAH on Córdoba Street. I was around there, very young, recently graduated, when someone said, "Pedro Armillas is downstairs." Then I took a copy of my thesis, because I had just graduated, and I saw this man coming up the stairs. He looked like a faun. I saw this faun with a beard, his forehead very wrinkled, with an enormous pipe. I identified with him automatically, and thought, "This is the man." And I gave him my thesis. He didn't know who I was. I said to him: "Dr. Armillas, I want to introduce myself, I am Eduardo Matos, this is the thesis I have just finished presenting, I would like you to read it."

He responded: "Of course, of course, I'll be glad to."

And off he went. Afterward we hardly ever saw each other. He was in Chicago, I was in Mexico. But I always had a high regard for that man who had fought in the war, and for the man who had taken an innovative position in archaeology. He had a number of followers, like William Sanders and others.

D: Do you have any particular memories of Pedro Armillas?

E: One day that was very important to me was the day he sent me a letter. I was in my office. This was when I was beginning my life as a bureaucrat in archaeology. I had already become an assistant director of Pre-hispanic Monuments. This post was offered to me in 1967 by Dr. Eusebio Dávalos, director of the INAH. I came in as assistant to Marquina, who was already a grand old man of nearly eighty years of age. The work with him was not very difficult. Shortly afterward I was named director of Pre-hispanic Monuments in 1974 or 1975. So anyway, one day I was in my office and they told me, "A gentleman wants to see you," and in comes this huge young man, big, very tall. And I thought, "What does this guy want?" He had a letter from Pedro Armillas, and I took it and read it. In the letter Pedro told me, "Eduardo, I am recommending this person to you very highly, because he is a student in Chicago, a student whom I am directing. Help him. He wants to spend a few nights in Tula, Teotihuacan, and other sites like Xochicalco." So then I looked way up to see the fellow and told him: "Well, listen. Sit down. You want to go to these places?"

"Yes."

That man was Davíd Carrasco, no less. I thought, "Well, what do you know! This youngster wants to go out there at night. Well, OK. The mosquitoes will eat him." We set it up, and that was my first contact with Davíd Carrasco.

D: Did we talk about Eliade at that time?

E: Yes, because you were a follower of Eliade. I was then publishing my book *Death by Obsidian Knife* where I mentioned Eliade. Chapter 2 of that book talks about the analysis of myths. I didn't know what a myth was, then I began to read. And I read Lévi-Strauss, Eliade, Otto, and so on, scholars of religion, trying to learn what a myth was and how it worked in culture. Eliade was also, by a strange coincidence, my point of contact with you, a student of Eliade's and Armillas's.

I remember one time when I was in Palenque. I had been sent to Palenque because there was going to be a presidential visit or something. I used to climb up to the top of the tomb at Palenque, the Temple of the Inscriptions, and sit there alone watching the evening fall. Thinking over the afternoon, those sorts of thoughts. And one day Pedro Armillas and his wife arrived in a little white sports car. I invited Pedro to come up there one evening, and we sat on the edge of the stairway in the upper part of the temple. We were looking out into space, Pedro with a red bandana tied on his forehead, his pipe, and I also with a pipe. Suddenly I asked him: "Pedro, you are a person who has worked and contributed a lot to Mesoamerican archaeology and all. Wouldn't you someday like to, sort of between work and rest, come out here to Palenque and excavate the *pelota* court or some other structure?"

"Well, sure. Yes it would be interesting, of course. . . ."

We talked about different things while the evening fell. He was only there for a couple of days. But it was a great experience to be there with the elderly Armillas. Later, I remember very clearly when we organized the first conference in Colorado in 1979, and there was Pedro, with his yellow sweater and his pipe. And shortly after he returned to Chicago, we heard of his death. He had gone out walking and suffered a heart attack. The news was terrible for us in Mexico. I remember that a tribute to honor him was organized immediately in the National Museum of Anthropology. José Luis Lorenzo, Teresa Rojas, and I spoke. We talked about the many diverse facets of his life.

The tribute I delivered there was later published through a university in the southern United States. But Armillas, in short, well he was a very important figure for me, and he still is.

D: Between the time you handed him your thesis and the day I arrived at your office, did Armillas have a detailed knowledge of your work? Does your understanding of his theories come from classes you took with him, or only from reading his articles? I ask because Armillas was very familiar with your work and mentioned the importance of your writing and scholarship to me.

E: I was never directly a student of his. Our relationship was always by means of chats, my reading of his work and my work that I sent to him, nothing more. There was never a more formal relationship.

D: So, it is interesting that many years later you and I have dedicated our book *The Great Temple of Tenochtitlan* to Mircea Eliade and Pedro Armillas, and have combined our work in this way.

E: Exactly. It is very significant in both those ways. And also very significant in the sense—I don't know for you, but at least for me—that one of them represented materialism, or that aspect of a duality. One was a man who had fought, a man wounded in his body, in short, a man who supported this view. On the other hand there was an individual immersed in the study of religion who tended toward archetypal views. This duality that is in me as well. I don't know how you experienced this presence.

D: Well, this presence for me was also very important because it seemed to me the more I became familiar with Mesoamerica, the more I realized that the crucial evidence in the study of Mesoamerican religion was embedded in archaeology. And while many colleagues in religious studies study scripts and books, in Mesoamerica you have this material world examined by archaeology that was so fundamental. So Armillas led me to you, and you led me to the Templo Mayor, and then Eliade was there in my background providing a sense of the imagination of all this. So, I think in a sense our duality is reflected in that duality.

E: Exactly. I believe these have been two very important presences in my life, and from what I have seen, in yours as well.

Archaeological movements in Mexico

D: More or less on the same subject, we'd like to hear something about the movements, the theories you thought about in those years of your education. For example, when I studied in the divinity school at the University of Chicago, the dominant movement was the study of myth to understand the fundamental essence of *homo religiosus*. But during the time I was there it changed somewhat because a stronger emphasis on ritual came in. Some scholars held that rituals are more basic than myths and a controversy arose that continues today. On one side was Eliade, on the other Jonathan Smith or Victor Turner. This was very interesting for us. In your case, what were the most important movements and disputes in the discourse of anthropology and archaeology?

E: In the seventies, when I was studying and beginning my professional career in the INAH, there were no movements or schools of thought as such in archaeology, but rather personal positions within the discipline. For example, in those years there was a very marked presence of two leaders within archaeology; José Luis Lorenzo on the one hand and Román Piña Chan on the other. They held very different views. Lorenzo was strongly influenced by Gordon Childe, which I found very persuasive since Childe's postulates seemed very useful for understanding the development of past societies, seen from the point of view of a process of evolution-revolution, that is, quantitative and qualitative changes. Piña Chan, on the other hand, had a profound understanding of Mesoamerican cultures and the phases of their ceramics, and a sociological view of archaeology that is evident in some of his writing. Still, he tended to favor the reconstruction of buildings once they were excavated, and I was not in agreement with that. Lorenzo gave a great boost to archaeological research by founding the Laboratories of Prehistory in the early seventies, with specialists like biologists, geologists, paleontologists, chemists, and so on, while Piña continued to take a more traditional view.

There was also a difference in their techniques of archaeological excavation. Lorenzo was very strict and careful to make sure that the boundaries of the area to be excavated were precisely located; that an accounting and registry of the recovered materials was kept. By contrast, Piña Chan excavated intuitively based on his enormous experience in the field, but wasn't so rigid as to archaeological verification.

L: So what impact did Lorenzo and Piña Chan have on your generation? How did they influence your own work?

E: You see the presence of each in the people they taught. I don't think—and I have written about this—that the researchers taught by Lorenzo fully understood the thinking of Gordon Childe. So, I wouldn't say there was really a specific movement established. But there wasn't on the side of Piña Chan either, except for studies focused on ceramic seriation or on the reconstruction of monuments. So there was not really any movement to follow. Because I was influenced by Marxism, I tended toward the ideas of Childe, which had been introduced in Mexico by Pedro Armillas. I wouldn't call him a Marxist, but certainly a scholar with a more social orientation toward archaeology. I found myself practically alone. There were scholars like Julio César Olivé or Roger Bartra who held a Marxist view of history. I could see that many Marxist postulates, above all historical materialism, could be applied usefully to archaeology. I had to practically teach myself by reading the works of Marx, Engels, Childe himself, or Hosbaum and Godelier, I mean the work of people who took a materialist approach to history. My thesis was a combination of the ideas of Childe and Marxism, so much so that it was entitled "The Urban Revolution in the Valley of Mexico."

L: Have there been times in your career when these ideas or principles have been questioned?

E: Yes, when I had to confront the reality of applying a historical materialist view to a concrete case: the Templo Mayor of the Aztecs. I came to realize that Marxism paid a great deal of attention to such areas as the economy, technology, division of social classes, and so forth, but very little to superstructural aspects like religion, myths, rituals, and so on, which I now confronted and which were present in the Templo Mayor. I realized that those things were present and that I was not dealing with just a religious building, but that a lot more was involved. In spite of this, I did apply some concepts of historical materialism such as conceiving that the gods who presided in the Templo Mayor had a relation to the economic structure. At that time, around 1978, there were studies by scholars of religion available and I had to look to them to understand the problem I was facing. Books by Mircea Eliade, Alfredo López Austin, my conversations with Davíd Carrasco, and so on, were very helpful in opening a new perspective on the phenomenon of religion. This was enriched by readings of Mauss, Otto, Lévi-Strauss, and other religious scholars.

I was very pleased to find that many of the postulates of Eliade came to life in the Templo Mayor. The relationship of historical reality-myth-ritual is present there. The temple as a sacred space in contrast to profane spaces, as the center of the universe, was also evident. The cyclical concept and the myth of eternal return are also embodied there.

And all this without overlooking how the economic maintenance of Tenochtitlan depended on the presence of those two gods in the upper part of the temple. That's why I had to take my own pathway, since my Marxist friends like Mario Sanoja, Luis Lumbreras, Felipe Bate, or Julio Montané couldn't give me much help. They were immersed in other kinds of problems.

To finish with this subject I should tell you that in 1979 I wrote an article entitled "Archaeological Movements in Mexico" in an anthology that I prepared about Marxist thought and materialism in archaeology for the journal *Nueva Antropología*. I included works by Miguel Othón de Mendizábal, Pedro Armillas, Roger Bartra, the results of the 1975 meeting in Teotihuacan, works by Enrique Nalda, Juan Yadeun, and two of my own pieces. In the article I mentioned earlier I concluded that there had been three movements in Mexican archaeology: one which tended toward the monumental reconstruction of buildings without specific theoretical principles; the technicist, with people who were preoccupied by the techniques of excavation, as in the case of Lorenzo; and the Marxist, which had very few adherents, and was really almost nonexistent but for a few notable exceptions. I don't think this has changed much. Though certain new movements have arisen on the international level, they are scarcely reflected in our archaeology. If we were to ask Mexican archaeologists what movement or school they belong to, I think very few could answer that question.

L: The great archaeologists of the twentieth century have had their particular interests, their thematic focuses and theoretical perspectives. There is, for example Kent Flannery's interest in the first villages and the origins of agriculture, or Sanders and Parsons who were more interested in surface surveys with ecological and regional scopes.. In your case, I see a constant interest in the great capitals of central Mexico: Cholula, Tenochtitlan, Tula, and Tlatelolco. And in each of these cases not only do you focus on the urban centers, but also on the ceremonial centers, the symbolic places in those cities. What can you tell us about that? Why that particular interest? After such extensive experience, what are your thoughts about the religion and the urban world of Mesoamerica?

E: Many years ago I was interviewed and it was pointed out to me that certain archaeological sites were identified with a particular archaeologist who had excavated there. For example, Monte Albán with Caso, Teotihuacan with Manuel Gamio, and they named two or three other sites where this identification of an ancient city with an archaeologist existed. At that time I was identified with Tenochtitlan and more specifically with the Templo Mayor as a sacred space. From that perspective, I think my interest dates from when I was a student of archaeology. First, I had the opportunity to work in different cities in central Mexico like Teotihuacan, Cholula, Tula, Tlatelolco, and Tenochtitlan. This aroused my interest in studying the importance of ceremonial centers and their relation to the sacred. The ideas of Eliade were important in analyzing the sacred spaces of the cities without losing sight of what he refers to as profane spaces. One has to understand that a city has a sacred character, but inside it there is a space of supreme holiness, the center of centers, as I have called it. I recognized the importance of being able to study these places which have the character of centers, of *axis mundi*, where we find the principal temple which unites the celestial level with the underworld and from which the four directions of the universe extend. The temple is the sacred space par excellence. The diverse forces converge in it.

The experience of having worked in the ceremonial areas of all these ancient cities was useful when I dealt with the Aztec Templo

Mayor. In my study I applied two categories: phenomenon and essence. The first corresponds to what is evident: the architecture, the gods who preside over it, the feasts and ceremonies that are celebrated in it. The second, the essence, refers to what is not evident, to what surrounds the building. For example, how the gods relate to the economic, political, and social systems. It was not just a religious building with gods in the upper part; rather there was a whole series of interrelated aspects that had to be explained.

Now, the rise of the city, the metropolis, is a phenomenon that archaeology has yet to explain. The discussion is ongoing. We have the case of Teotihuacan, which is the first great city of central Mexico. Why did Teotihuacan form? Ideas come and go, but we still do not have an adequate explanation. I myself have proposed some possible explanations for the rise and fall of Teotihuacan, but they are hypotheses that are not fully proven. The alpha and omega of cities is a stirring question that has not yet been answered.

L: When you talk now about the rise and fall of cities, several decades after your work on Teotihuacan started, what are your conclusions? Of course, nobody has the complete answer to the rise and fall of Teotihuacan, but from your vantage point, what are some of the likely principal causes for the rise of this unique urban phenomenon in Mesoamerica? Above all, I would like to hear your hypothesis about the causes of the collapse of the city, and what you disagree with in other hypotheses.

E: The rise is always more problematical. Whoever has written about the rise of cities, like Gordon Childe with his "urban revolution," or Paul Wheatley in the case of Asian cities, has confronted similar problems. In the specific case of Teotihuacan we have some antecedents like Tlapacoya, Copilco, Cerro del Tepalcate, Terremote, Cuicuilco, and others. All of these were sited near Lake Texcoco and although they depended on agriculture, they made use of the lake's resources: plants, fish, and waterfowl. Cuicuilco is a special case, since it was destroyed by lava from the volcano Xitle. Some authors have suggested that, faced with this natural disaster, the population migrated a few kilometers to the north to settle in Teotihuacan, where we know there had been an earlier settlement.

Teotihuacan is located in a place that has useful resources. There is raw material for construction and the making of tools, like the nearby deposits of obsidian. It also has rivers and something I consider very important: year-round springs. From this I constructed what I called the "green area" hypothesis. It depends on taking advantage of these springs which, once they are channeled, allow considerable agricultural production. Where there are no great rivers like the ones that supported cultures in Egypt or Mesopotamia, these springs are indispensable for agriculture. They are depicted in the murals of Tepantitla where one sees this spring from which the current of water flows, and how it is channeled and how they build a *chinampa*, a type of garden plot, where corn and other plants are grown. For an agricultural people, having water that flows out of the earth has not only a symbolic character relating to the god of water, but also with appropriate technology they could have garden plots to cultivate. I covered the southern area of the town of San Juan Teotihuacan and I found these parcels bordered by canals. I saw the same thing in Cholula, which was contemporaneous with Teotihuacan. We did surveys with aerial photography and we found springs that welled up very near the great pyramid and flowed to the south. Pictographs from the sixteenth century also indicate how a stream of water flows from the great pyramid at Cholula. The name "green areas" that I gave to this hypothesis refers directly to the fact that these areas with perennial springs remain green all year thanks to the presence of water and humidity.

The rapid growth of Teotihuacan is surprising, and no doubt something similar happened in Cholula. As a result of this growth and owing to other factors as well, we note a regional ruralization perhaps provoked by the presence of the city, which absorbs and attracts population. Now, we must clarify something about the "green areas" hypothesis: in the beginnings of the cities the springs played an essential role, but as the cities grew it is obvious that greater production was required. So in addition to exploiting the area of the springs, they had to expand into other agricultural regions or impose tribute upon conquered peoples to supplement their own production.

L: And what can you say about the collapse?

E: Various ideas have been suggested on this subject, from the idea that it might have been an epidemic that decimated the population, to the idea that strong earthquakes might have caused their flight. The truth is that no archaeological evidence has been found to support these ideas. There are no great cracks in the buildings or anything like that. For his part, Jaime Litvak has proposed that toward the end of Teotihuacan new centers arose which cut off their commercial relations, so that the city was progressively strangled. There has also been a Marxist interpretation offered, that is, that there was a rebellion by the working classes against an elite that flaunted its power. And of course, we have heard the idea that massive harvesting of wood and other resources caused an ecological problem, which is contradicted by the research that has been done on the flora of the locality.

For my part, I have proposed another alternative. To support it, I started with evidence that seems to confirm that Teotihuacan was a militaristic society and not, as was thought for so many years, only theocratic. Not only do we find warriors in the murals, but we also see some regions that they must have controlled militarily. That is true of part of the present-day state of Hidalgo, where there are deposits of obsidian like the Cerro de las Navajas. Obsidian is the fundamental raw material for the making of tools, weapons, and symbolic objects.

There are also deposits of limestone, which are needed to make the stucco that covered the buildings. Teotihuacan used enormous quantities of this material. A society like that of Teotihuacan, with a population that made it the largest city in Mesoamerica, whose presence was felt throughout Mesoamerica, cannot be understood to have been governed only by priests. I think that in Teotihuacan we already have the duality of priest and warrior, fulfilling the two fundamental requirements of this society: the ideological aspect controlled by the priests, and the repressive aspect controlled by the military. We should not forget that Sanders has discovered sites five kilometers away from Teotihuacan where weapons were produced. And a route from Teotihuacan through the region of Tlaxcala shows some defenses built against the expansion of the city. The discoveries made in the Temple of Quetzalcóatl and recently in the Pyramid of the Moon seem to indicate that there were sacrifices of humans who were possibly prisoners of war. In short, I think there are many indications that show Teotihuacan would have had this theocratic-military character.

Based on all this, I suggested that what might have happened was that some moment of weakness in the control exerted by Teotihuacan over the groups that were conquered and subject to tribute might have allowed an uprising against the city. This would finally result in the burning of Teotihuacan and the dispersion of the inhabitants.

I also base this on the fact that we see these uprisings against centralized power on a number of occasions in the history of central Mexico after the fall of Teotihuacan. This may have been the case in Tula; in the well known case of Azcapotzalco, where they controlled several groups, like the Aztecs or Mexicas, and in a moment of internal problems in Azcapotzalco, the conquered and tributary groups rebelled against the metropolis. We all know the result: the Tepanecas of Azcapotzalco were defeated by their ancient vassals. The same thing happened shortly afterward: the Mexicas controlled numerous tributary groups that allied themselves with the Spanish in order to liberate themselves from Tenochtitlan. We also know the outcome: the Aztecs were defeated by their former subjects and the Spanish forces. History repeated itself.

So, all of this leads me to suggest that something similar must have happened in Teotihuacan.

D: Excellent. Why don't we come at this question of your thinking from another angle? Your publications, for example. I remember that my first publication was a review. I was very worried that the publisher wouldn't accept it, but fortunately they did. What were your first publications? What was their focus? I'm thinking of your publications previous to *Death by Obsidian Knife*, because that book combines Marxism and religious history.

E: Well. I remember that my first article was published in the journal, *Tlatoani*, which was the publication of the alumni society of ENAH. It was about the dwellings of the rural population in pre-hispanic Mexico. It's a subject that had not had much attention before then, so I was immediately interested since it dealt with the dwellings of the majority of the population. I mentioned how there were wealthy people living in Lomas de Chapultepec, while poor people were living in caves. It was a very basic social criticism, of course, but it showed my way of thinking at the time. Later I published an article in the *Anales del INAH*, entitled "El adoratorio decorado de las calles de Argentina" based on a salvage excavation which I directed right in the center of Mexico City. Another article also in *Anales* was "La danza de los Montezumas," a dance that is still danced in the Republic of Panama, which began my interest in contemporary popular expressions. Those were my first publications. As to my first book, that was *Death by Obsidian Knife*, published in 1975 in the series SEPsetentas. It has been reprinted six times by the Fondo de Cultura Económica. In that book, for sure, you see a Marxist approach as you said and the thinking of several scholars of religion, like Eliade. It was a preamble to what would come next in the Templo Mayor. That would take the form of another book: *Life and Death in the Templo Mayor*.

I think we should take a more profound look at this subject of death, which interests and excites me. This began at the time when Leonardo López Luján found the ceramic sculptures of the gods of death, the Mictlantecuhtli, in the northern part of the Templo Mayor. In his study, the analysis of these figures draws him deeply into the subject and gives some very interesting insights into ritual death at the Templo Mayor. All of this made me reflect that it was necessary to look more profoundly into the subject of death. It gives me pleasure to recall that on one occasion Guillermo Bonfil, the noted social anthropologist, commented that the only specific writing about the subject of death was the book by Eduardo Matos that had just come out in SEPsetentas. In fact, scholars had dealt with certain aspects of death among the Aztecs, like Alfonso Caso, discussing the subject along with other aspects of the life of that people. On the other hand, it was strange that the first book I wrote was not about archaeology, but about death in pre-hispanic Mexico, which I still find profoundly interesting. I should say that in 1972, in the same series SEPsetentas, I had published an anthology of the works of Manuel Gamio, an anthropologist for whom I feel an enormous admiration. It was entitled *Manuel Gamio, arqueología e indigenismo*. Many consider him the father of Mexican anthropology with his vision of integrated projects that take into consideration two fundamental categories: population and territory.

The themes that I have given the most attention to in my academic life are already present in my first publications: the theme of death in pre-hispanic Mexico; the history of archaeology, with the biography I wrote for the anthology of Manuel Gamio; and the Templo Mayor of the Aztecs.

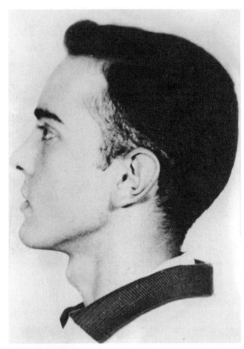

Fig 6. Eduardo joins INAH in 1960.

Fig 7. Eduardo Matos and his schoolmate Pablo López at INAH in 1960.

Fig 8. Talking with the physical anthroplogist Arturo Romano in the old National Museum in 1962.

Fig 9. Eduardo with colleagues in the Café Moneda at the School of Anthropology in Mexico City. Left to right are Angel García Cook, Jesús Montoya, Juan Luna, Andrés Medina, and Eduardo, 1961.

Fig 10. Eduardo assisting in the transport of a Maya sculpture in Malpaso, Chiapas, 1966.

Fig 11. A closeup of Eduardo assisting in the transport of a Maya sculpture in Malpaso, Chiapas, 1966.

Fig 12. Eduardo Matos
excavating in 1963

Fig 13. Excavating in the Palace of
the Butterflies, Teotihuacan while
assisting Jorge Acosta, 1963.

Fig 14. Excavating in the Palace of the Butterflies in Teotihuacan in 1963.

Fig 15. Eduardo Matos with the art historian George Kubler at Yale University in 1983.

CHAPTER FOUR

The Templo Mayor Project

THE SECOND BREAKING POINT:
FROM PRESIDENT TO COYOLXAUHQUI

D: WE HAVE SEEN THAT THERE HAVE BEEN certain breaking points that have brought about transformations and enriched your life. We talked about your experience of stuttering and your childhood in Santo Domingo. What other breaking points have had an impact on your career or on other aspects of your life?

E: To recapitulate, the first great breaking point in my life that I confronted alone, all by myself, was with religion, which we already talked about. This breaking point at fifteen years of age made me feel like a man who was free from a series of prejudices, ideas which at that time I felt I had discarded. The second great breaking point came with the power that one can achieve inside the archaeological endeavor. It is important here to talk about what led up to this breaking point. I want to emphasize that for me each one of these breaking points further enriched and strengthened a series of internal thoughts and signified steps in a creative process. I mean, for me one has to know how to make each breaking point lead to a new creative stage in life. The second breaking point resulted from several causes. First, my bureaucratic life inside archaeology had been developing quite well—quite well within the necessary limitations that are archaeological bureaucracy. That is, the necessity of having to take care of affairs as director of Pre-hispanic Monuments, and later as president of the Council of Archaeology and leaving research aside to some extent. Although really I never left it aside; I always kept publishing even though I had a lot of administrative duties.

It happened that in 1975 I was named by the general director of the INAH, Guillermo Bonfil, to head the department of Pre-hispanic Monuments. Shortly afterward there was a change in INAH and Dr. Gastón García Cantú became the director. He named me president of the Council of Archaeology. This happened in early 1977. This is the highest position in our national archaeology. I replaced a great archaeologist, Dr. Ignacio Bernal, who had held the post for several years. At thirty-six years of age, I was very young when I arrived there, and I was very pleased to have been given the position. I had reached the highest position after having held the posts of director of ENAH, associate director and then director of Pre-hispanic Monuments, and also secretary of the Mexican Society of Anthropology.

Even so, I wasn't altogether satisfied. I felt something important was missing. Since I had had such a rapid rise as a bureaucrat, I felt unfulfilled as a researcher. I felt that I needed to do research, publish more, in short to dedicate myself fully to academic work. So I made an important decision. About six months had passed when I began to feel more and more unsatisfied with myself, despite having such eminent councilors on the Council as Alberto Ruz, José Luis Lorenzo, and Augusto Molina and an entire group of very outstanding people in the field of archaeology. At that time I was offered the leadership of the project in Tikal, in Guatemala. I thought deeply about whether to accept it or not, about what I was going to do. Then I made a decision: to go and talk to the general director of the Institute and tell him that I no longer wanted to be president of the Council of Archaeology. That was my second breaking point. It took place, if I remember correctly, in August of 1977. I spoke with Gastón García Cantú and said: "Professor, I am very grateful to you for naming me to the post, but I have been thinking and truthfully I want to resign and return to full-time research."

Don Gastón understood immediately, and reminded me that it was an extremely important post that many people wanted but that after all he did understand if I wanted to go back to research. He asked to delay my departure until he could become acquainted with the institute and the archaeologists to see who he should name in my place. I also told him that if I made this change, I wanted to finish my doctoral thesis. We came to an agreement. I consider this my second breaking point because it was a position of power within the archaeological establishment. One decides, in conjunction with the Council, whether a project will be approved or not: whether it will be funded, and so on. Even so, I threw this overboard, that is, I broke with this administrative power in my discipline to dedicate myself to research. I reaffirmed my break with enormous administrative power years later in 2000, when Sari Bermúdez, president of the National Council of Culture and Arts invited me to become director of the INAH and I didn't accept. I felt that the proper time to be general director had passed. My priority continued to be research and writing.

D: During those months did you feel better or were you still unsatisfied? How did you feel after resigning?

E: I continued as president for about six or seven months, up until early 1978, to give García Cantú time to decide who he would name. But I was already sure I would leave the Council, that my decision had been accepted, and that I would dedicate myself to research. For that reason, I was a bit more satisfied with myself for having made the break despite the accompanying loss of power within the discipline.

Then came the year of 1978, a transcendent year in my life. In January Professor García Cantú let me know that he had decided who would replace me as president of the Council, Professor José Luis Lorenzo. The change was made in January, and I began to represent INAH at an archaeological convention in Panama. I went to Panama and was there for a week. Coming back, in the airport at Tocumen in Panama, I boarded the airplane. It was a Mexican airline, and I picked up a Mexican newspaper and read about a great discovery in the Zócalo, "An important Aztec sculpture found!" And I thought, "Well, journalists always exaggerate." I didn't pay much attention to it. When I got back to Mexico City, it was a Saturday, I got home, and the first thing my wife said was: "Listen, the people from the institute are looking for you, they want you to call, to go there on Monday. They say it's very important."

I went to INAH and on the stairs I met a secretary who immediately told me: "Professor, it's good you're here. We have been looking for you."

"But I was out of the country at a convention."

"Well, go on in, go ahead. Professor García Cantú is waiting for you."

When I entered the office García Cantú, who was presiding over a meeting, stood up immediately and said: "Eduardo, It's a good thing you're here. Have you already been in Guatemala?"

"No, professor, I was in Panama."

"No, in Guatemala Street!"

And I said: "No, why? What's going on?"

"An extremely important sculpture has been discovered. That's why we're meeting. Come. Sit down, because we are going to authorize the funding for the entire excavation project."

D: So all the archaeologists who belonged to the Council were in that meeting?

E: Yes, they were. Lorenzo, who I mentioned was the president of the Council, was there. The archaeologist García Cook, who was director of Salvage Archaeology. People from the Department of the Distrito Federal, which was going to supply the funding. The architect Carlos

Chanfón who was the director of Colonial Monuments. That's where they agreed on how much funding there would be. It's interesting to note that a month earlier, when we were discussing my resignation, Don Gastón had asked me: "Eduardo, now that you are leaving the Council what do you want to do?"

"Well, look, I want to write my doctoral thesis and also to go to Tepeapulco, which is an important site, to do a surface survey with a student of mine."

"I have a better offer for you. There is a plan to work in the center of the city. Would you like to take charge of that?"

"Yes, of course. I have always been interested in Tenochtitlan, and even more in the center of the city. I'd love to."

It so happened that one month later the discovery of the huge stone carving of the Aztec goddess Coyolxauhqui was made in the very heart of Mexico City. That's why Don Gastón wanted to see me, because he had offered me the leadership of the project if it went forward . . . and suddenly there was this very important discovery.

D: What did you observe the first time you came face to face with Coyolxauhqui?

E: I went to Guatemala Street where the Salvage Archaeology team from INAH was doing its work with Coyolxauhqui. I stepped in and saw that enormous statue, more than 3 meters in diameter, the figure of a naked woman with the body mutilated, the legs and the arms separated from the torso, decapitated. In short, it was impressive as much for its size and quality as for its importance and meaning. As I said, Salvage Archaeology was working on this. They continued to find certain offerings and I had already begun to plan what would be the excavation of the Templo Mayor de Tenochtitlan. I want to point out here something very important because it relates to what the Templo Mayor meant to me. I consider it to be one of the most important aspects of my life: the Templo Mayor was the place where the academic necessities I felt took shape, and which led me to break with the Council of Archaeology. I mean, I had the full support of the general director of INAH and the Council of Archaeology to allow me to carry out the archaeological work in the way that I was planning it. I was able to fully develop my ideas of how an interdisciplinary research project in an urban environment, in downtown Mexico City, like the Templo Mayor, should be done.

The work was carried out with extreme rigor in the excavation of the Templo Mayor area and in each offering. It was a unique case in Mesoamerican archaeology, since there were offerings that, because of the care with which they were handled, their complexity and so on, required three to eight months of excavation. I had seen how my colleagues from Salvage Archaeology had initially excavated some of the offerings around the Coyolxauhqui sculpture, and it was disastrous. The information, the data, was lost. There was one of them, already a great archaeologist, whose name I prefer not to mention, who even called [the offerings] the "leftovers." So their strategy was just get the leftovers out of the way, get them out, like that . . . a horrible thing. Under my direction we were careful to exercise extreme rigor. And that rigor has made it possible now, after years have passed, for other researchers who do studies of the offerings, of the temple, to count on considerable precision. So, to make a long story short, I was able during those five years of excavation in that site, to develop my idea of what an archaeological excavation is. My collaborators helped me in this. I have very fond memories of Paco Hinojosa, Juan Alberto Román, Isabel Gutiérrez, Pilar Luna, Eduardo Contreras, Diana Wagner, and Salvador Guilliem, who began as a photographer and ended up an archaeologist, Carlos González, Bertina Olmedo, Elsa Hernández, and a sixteen-year-old Leonardo López Luján, who was the best at turning in the weekly reports. As time went by, we added new generations of archaeologists like Adrián Velázquez, Diego

Jiménez Badillo, Ximena Chávez, Álvaro Barrera, it would be hard to name them all . . . As to art conservators, I had a number who were very good at their work: Bárbara Hasbach, María Luisa Franco, Vida Mercado, Yolanda Santaella, Nishimura. . . . . And of course the biologists like Oscar Polaco and later Aurora Montúfar. We also had the support of the Laboratorios de Prehistoria and their specialists.

The three phases of the project

D: How did you organize the project?

E: I divided the project into three phases: first the collection of information that was known previous to our project, coming from archaeological work and from historical sources. On the one hand, information from archaeologists like Gamio, Batres, and others who had worked in the same area decades before and on the other, information from sixteenth-century written sources, Sahagún, Durán, Tezozómoc, writers who described the Templo Mayor to us.

So these two large areas of knowledge, archaeology and history, were elements that allowed us to gain a profound knowledge of the precursors and characteristics of the Templo Mayor. We were in a position to confirm this knowledge through archaeology.

There were some archaeologists who criticized and said, "But why make this expenditure? Why excavate the temple, when we have written sources that tell us what was there?" They didn't understand that sources can be very relative; that the perception of an individual can color what he sees and how he describes it, in this case the Templo Mayor. But he may change his attitude toward what he sees or interpret it from a personal viewpoint. It has to be confirmed archaeologically. And that is what we did. So, in the first phase we compiled all the existing information about the Templo Mayor and based our plans and ideas on it. The second phase was the excavation: five years of constant work in the heart of Mexico City, with all the academic and social experience that implies. And finally, the third phase; the interpretation. That is, analyzing the materials we found to produce our conclusions. This is something that had not been done in other important projects of Mexican archaeology, so there was not much information about the results. We wanted to change that practice, which we didn't consider very professional, and to make our results widely known, and finish the project with the interdisciplinary participation of ethnohistorians, specialists in colonial subjects, archaeologists, chemists, and biologists, among others. So, from the standpoint of academic practices, the project was extremely important.

The third breaking point: the family

D: As I understand it, it was a thoroughly satisfying time academically, but what importance did the Templo Mayor project have for the other part of your duality, for your internal and spiritual world?

E: In my internal world it was also satisfying, because the farther I advanced in the excavation, the more certain I felt that I was filling an academic need. I felt secure enough to begin reviewing what my life up to then had been. Then something very interesting happened. The farther the excavation went, the more I progressed in finding the remains of the Templo Mayor, the more I found myself. I mean, the more I was able to observe myself, to analyze myself. The Templo Mayor allowed me that security, and also allowed me to make this profound analysis of my life. This led to my third breaking point: the break with my family.

This breaking point manifested itself this way: in 1968 I had married María Eugenia del Valle Prieto, a very intelligent, cultured woman. But it came out in my self-evaluation that this marriage coincided with my period as a bureaucrat, with my rise in the administrative world of archaeology. She fit that time and she fit it very well. We had two children, Daniela and Eduardo. I lived with her for thirteen years. But the time came when I felt an inner void, the same way I had felt something lacking in my academic life.

D: Was she an archaeologist or scholar?

E: She is an anthropologist. So then, my analysis allowed me to see with complete clarity that she belonged to that period of my administrative ascent. Her presence was very important, but I never allowed her into that interior world of mine, the world of the fifteen- or sixteen-year-old, the world of my feelings, my emotions at the fall of evening. She belonged more to a material world which was reflected in the sense of "the good life." We lived in an enormous, marvelous house. My library was 25 meters long, there was a colonial fountain outside my room, a marvelous view. And yet, I left all that. I had to confront it and find the courage to leave all that materiality. I had to leave a very fine woman and also leave my children, because logically, they stayed with their mother, although I continued to see them. But we know what that means. This breaking point, which I call the break with the family, a break with something that was well established, was a transformative step. It became a third breaking point that would also lead to creative elements.

D: Eduardo, as I listen to your narration of these three breaking points in your life, I notice certain coincidences that may reveal a pattern. For example, at the same time when the discovery of Coyolxauhqui, a sculpture of a sacrificed and mutilated woman, is made in your professional life, you renounce the woman in your personal life. Another coincidence is that during the period when you are excavating the Templo Mayor you are likewise excavating yourself, searching for your internal center. This reminds me of a theme in the work of Eliade, where he postulates that man always thirsts or hungers to find his center. In your life there are periods when you are not centered, but one way or another you always seek and rediscover your center. . . . We could look at your life as an interior pilgrimage toward a center.

E: I really like that term you have used, the "pilgrimage toward a center." In fact, I do believe that's what a person's life is to some degree, a pilgrimage toward something. In my case, in my lifetime I had been closer or farther away from my center. So, the Templo Mayor gave me the opportunity to return to my interior center, but at the same time I was excavating the center of the universe of the Mexica society. Because for them, in the final analysis their conception of the Templo Mayor was just that: the center of centers, the place through which one ascended to the celestial level, and through which one descended to the underworld, from which the four cosmic directions were born, the four directions of the universe. Xiuhtecuhtli Huehueteotl, the ancient god who lives at the center of the universe, presided in this temple. So I had the opportunity to excavate the center of the Aztec universe. And at the same time as I was doing that, I was discovering hidden aspects of my own center.

So, what was this encounter with my own center? I remembered and reflected upon what my life had been. That is when I came to realize that in my family life, I was distant from the center of what I wanted deep inside. So what happened? We return again to the women. That dismembered woman in the stone, that woman who was my wife, and a new woman who appeared. This new woman came to the temple one day and was working on the stone image of the dismembered woman. That is, they were together because the new woman is a restorer, a conservator, and her task was to conserve the enormous sculpture of the mutilated goddess. One day, when those two women were there together, I went out. I was going to inspect the excavation, and suddenly I saw a blue flash of lightning.

That's how I thought of it at that moment. She turned to look at me, and that glance, her blue-green eyes, dazzled me. I mean I felt it like a blue flash of lightning which stunned me. From that moment there was no doubt because she and I both thought in that moment, "this person has to be mine, we have to be together." Then I went to talk to her next to that mutilated goddess. This was very important because I found my other half. I mean, this woman had the same feelings, the same appreciation for Rilke, a vision of life very similar to mine. We felt this affinity immediately. So we began to unite our lives under the Rilkean principle of being two solitudes who love each other, who revere each other, and become a unity without ceasing to be two.

From that moment, my life was enriched in a very significant way. I began to find the center of centers, my own center. To this was added the necessity of returning to my poetry, returning to doing sculpture. In short, it revived a number of things that I had given up for dead. I now began to feel the need to create again, and I began to do that along with her. We set up an atelier, a space of our own, where we would go every afternoon. There we would be, listening to the rain fall, drinking a good wine . . . and our companion was a mouse who suddenly ran through and disappeared into his hole. He was the only one who shared this world which was filled with our presence. This was also important and was one of the points that helped me to make the break. The years of excavation which we lived together were really an impressive experience. Each new discovery, each moment we spent together at work, those afternoons in our space with the classical music which always played . . . in short, we felt fully what now at last I understood was love. I believe that many talk about love, but few have experienced it. In this case I was able to live it and feel it completely.

We then began our travels overseas together. We went to Madrid, to Paris, always accompanying the relics of the Templo Mayor. It was in Paris where I wrote some thoughts that I entitled "Erectario," some fifteen short poems about a couple who meet, live out their sexuality fully until they become united and integrated on earth and in time.

We went to see the places Rilke had traveled. We were together in Ronda, a Spanish town where Rilke lived and wrote. I found out there that we were in Rilke's room, the room Rilke had occupied in the Reina Victoria Hotel. We were in Switzerland and went to the small town of Raron in the Alps, where he was buried. We went there on the train, and a curious thing happened. We were coming from Basel to Raron. When we were close to the stop where we were to get off and take another small train to Raron, suddenly, from high on the mountainside we saw a small church below, and at the same moment we both said, "That is the church where Rilke is buried." We knew it so well, that we carried it inside us. We finally arrived, and caught the small train that took us to that town and it turned out not to be a tourist town. It was a town with no taxis, there was nothing. There we were; I, a dark-skinned man with a large beard, and she, with a black cape. (I have always called her *la Bruja*, "the Witch" for her appearance.) So we walked through the streets, a witch and a faun . . . and the school children stood looking at us like we were strange creatures. We climbed up to the church where Rilke was buried. It was a very emotional moment. I cut and tied a lock of hair from my beard and she tied a lock of hair from her head to the rose bushes that grew alongside his tomb. Here's something interesting: Rilke died because he was scratched by a thorn on a rose bush and that accelerated a disease he already suffered from. And right there at his tomb there are roses. It was a grand moment being there among the Alps, that small village and close to Rilke.

D: Once when I was in the Templo Mayor, you gave me permission to visit the whole area. I came to a very protected area that had a drape covering an entrance. Behind it there was a man guarding a very impressive piece of white stone, with a strange design, about a meter and a half tall. You later told me it was one of your sculptures.

E: Yes, that's right, I managed to find a small space inside the excavation where I could carve that sculpture. I was helped by an old workman named Marcos. When you saw it, it was a small wooden room and the sculpture was an enormous vagina. It was a vagina with a base also of stone, and I called it somewhat jokingly and somewhat seriously "Paris, or where we come from and where we go." That's because they always used to say that children came from Paris. That sculpture was eventually shown by Belles Artes in the show for the Sculpture Triennial which was held around that time. I think it was 1981. That piece has also been mentioned in catalogs of sculpture and can be seen right now. It is in my brother's gallery, set in the central façade. As I said, I also did some in bronze and even some in stone and in plaster of Paris. So it was a time of poetic and sculptural creativity.

D: What impact does a sculpture in the shape of a vagina have on the people who visit your brother's gallery?

E: When it was exhibited in the Triennial, a woman came up with her daughter, a girl of some twelve or thirteen years. They stopped in front of it and stood looking at it. I moved a little closer to hear what they would say about it. Suddenly the girl asked: "Mama, what is that?"

The mother stood looking at the sculpture, looked closer, and then said: "Well, look, it appears to be the Virgin of Guadalupe, but without the Virgin."

D: I remember well that during my visits to the Templo Mayor there was an energy, an interest that you could feel in the air, in the people who were involved in the excavation, in the press, in the taxi drivers. There was a sort of electricity. It is clear that it had a great impact on Mexican culture, because Coyolxauhqui was printed on the covers of phone books and alongside the Templo Mayor on the paper currency. The significance of the excavation infiltrated Mexican imagery and art but also the consciousness of Mexican people. I remember well that the Templo Mayor has attracted many visitors from other states and other countries. In a sense it really was the discovery of the center of the world, and in a sense a new center, because there is Matos excavating, discovering a very ancient culture which had a certain image in the past, and now has a new one. With that in mind, I have a two-part question. The first part concerns these images which have had such an impact on the Republic of Mexico. The second, which I want you to answer in light of your duality, is this: what were the most important discoveries for you as regards their impact on our knowledge of the Aztecs, their history, and how have these discoveries changed that knowledge?

E: We should point out that during the period of excavation from 1978 to 1982 the Templo Mayor was the center of a lot of activity. It was the obligatory visit for important visitors. For example, the King and Queen of Spain, Margaret Thatcher, President Jimmy Carter were there, really it would be impossible to name all the important people who were there and whom I guided around. All of the presidents, prime ministers, and kings who visited Mexico. Three Nobel laureates for literature came there; Gabriel García Márquez, Octavio Paz, and Toni Morrison. Also artists like Jane Fonda and María Félix. A huge number of people wanted to see what was going on here. But perhaps the most important part of this was the population of the Distrito Federal itself and people from outside the city who took an interest in what was going on here. We were obliged to open the Templo Mayor on Saturdays so people could come in and observe what was being done (in a very restricted area, of course.) I have always said that an archaeological excavation is like the operating room of a surgeon, where members of the family should not be allowed to enter. There is the surgeon, in this case the archaeologists, and they are opening up this body. They are opening up the earth and penetrating with supreme caution, and there must not be any interference with this work. So we opened one part so it could be visited on Saturdays from 10:00 in the morning to noon. And we had an impressive number of people. There was an unbroken line. There were people, for example, who came from Monterrey and Puebla especially to get a look at what we were finding.

During those visits something very unusual happened. One Saturday we noticed that a young man had bent over toward the sculpture of Coyolxauhqui and put something down. I immediately ordered someone to see what it was, since there was a danger it might have been something destructive. This young man had placed a rose on the goddess. Something similar happened on another occasion, and I want to tell about it because it was very moving. We were presenting the exhibition in the palace of Bellas Artes, a grand exposition on the Templo Mayor which was attended by thousands and thousands of people. I had recommended to the director that great care be taken of two small sculptures of Xiuhtecuhtli, the fire god, because these two sculptures were shown on pedestals, but without protection, without the glass covers that protected the other pieces. So I asked her to arrange special vigilance so that they could not be touched or stolen. One day she called me at my office in the temple, crying, and said: "Eduardo, I called because something really amazing just happened . . ."

I immediately thought, "something got broken!" but she added:

"A guard just brought a bouquet of flowers to my office. It turns out that he was there watching when a woman wrapped in a shawl came in. When she arrived in front of one of the sculptures of Xiuhtecuhtli she crossed herself and knelt. When the guard saw this odd behavior, he moved closer and heard her say to the deity, 'you poor thing, how you have suffered, but now you are here.' She crossed herself again, pulled this bouquet from under her shawl and placed it at the feet of the sculpture."

I understood perfectly: I mean, I had seen it manifested in the young man's rose, in the bouquet of flowers, and in many other ways. It was the interest, and something else I can't quite define, which Mexican people feel about the pre-hispanic past. This affected me a lot. To sum up, the Templo Mayor became the center not only of the ancient Aztec empire, but also in a way a visitors' center . . . and not only for people of importance, but also for the common people.

At that time my image was also well known because the television crews came every day. It was in the news on Channel 2 every day. So of course, it made my face quite recognizable and sometimes, for example, when I went somewhere, maybe a restaurant or a store, I would be recognized immediately and they would start asking me about the excavation. They would ask what had we found, if there were any new offerings, and so on. This has served me well, too, because doctors and dentists don't charge me anything for their services; when they recognize me they immediately want to chat about archaeology. And once an odd thing happened to me: I was driving to the temple very early, at 7:00 in the morning, and my car broke down in Calzada de la Viga. I got out and hailed a cab. When I got in I told the driver: "Take me to the Zócalo."

When we were turning into Avenida 20 de Noviembre, which comes out at the Zócalo, the driver asked me: "Which side are you going to?"

"Over there where you see the yellow canvas."

You remember how we covered the whole site of excavation with huge yellow tarps. And the driver said: "Ah, the part where Matos is . . ."

And I answered: "Yes, but Matos is not there right now."

"Why not?"

"Because I'm here, it's me."

The guy didn't want to charge me. Of course I said: "Look, please, you have to charge me, this is your livelihood."

"No, no. I can't charge you."

"Well, then, we'll do this: invite your family, bring them here on Saturday, and I will show you around myself, so you can see what we're finding."

D: Why do you think these people react to you that way? For example, I think it's not just because you are well known, but also because they believe you are doing something that's important for everyone, for the Mexican people.

E: I think it is partly that, because on other occasions I have detected what you are talking about. For example, when people used to come to visit on Saturdays, I would ask them: "Well, what did you think of what you just saw, the Coyolxauhqui, the serpent heads?"

They would answer: "This is ours, what you are rescuing is something of ours."

On one occasion one of them even told me: "Professor, these are our roots, you must continue excavating. Tear down the cathedral and excavate under it, because there must be something very important there."

I answered: "Listen, that's the part of us that is Spanish, and besides that's a monument that one has to respect, it's a colonial monument."

"No, Professor. What's really ours is this."

The indigenous aspect is very deep in the Mexican character, along with a certain negativity toward the Spanish aspect. When a Mexican talks about the Conquest, he says, "They came and conquered us."

So who came to conquer? Your other part, isn't that right? Or part of your duality. This is a very strong feeling, and I believe people did feel that we were excavating the heart of a society, the center of its worldview. Another important thing: we were desanctifying archaeology to a degree. The archaeologist had always been viewed as a sage who excavated; nobody knew how he excavated, his results just showed up in a museum or a publication. But not here. Here people saw on a daily basis the care that has to be taken in an excavation, how it was a scientific labor, and how much those objects were valued. I think that was also very important to the people.

D: One of your workers told me that when President Carter visited the Templo Mayor, there was an interchange between you two about the depth of the excavation. Could you tell us about that?

E: Yes, in fact, President Carter and his wife visited Mexico and came to see the excavation of the Templo Mayor. On that day José López Portillo, the president of Mexico, came accompanying the North American president. That was during the "oil boom" when there was a lot of talk about the oil wealth of Mexico, so really, a rather idyllic image of our country. We were going through the excavation, and we came to a place where we had gone very deep with our test pits. I told President López Portillo: "Mr. President, I don't want to keep excavating here."

"But why, Professor?"

"If I keep digging, I just might strike oil."

He let out a great laugh, and they translated for President Carter who, to tell the truth, didn't find this very amusing.

D: But speaking of the Spanish influences in Mexico, help us imagine what impact visiting the Templo Mayor of the Aztecs had on the King and Queen of Spain.

E: Well, just think how hard it was for me to have to explain to the King of Spain that this was destroyed by his ancestors. It was rather difficult, but we made the tour at night. The area was illuminated, and it was really impressive. I think they did feel profoundly what this excavation signified. Especially the queen. I understand that Queen Sofía has a great interest in history and archaeology. I believe she took some courses in archaeology. Her interest was such that years later, in 1987, she made a quick 48-hour visit to Mexico. She was here to inaugurate something at the Red Cross, and as time was short, she was asked what she would like to visit during her stay besides attending the inauguration. The only thing she asked for was to come and see the museum of the Templo Mayor, because she had seen the excavations with the king, but now she wanted to see the museum and the artifacts. We took the tour, and she showed an impressive interest and what's more, it wasn't just a diplomatic sort of visit, or a visit for the sake of protocol. She really knew about the temple and asked me questions that showed she had read some about the temple. After her visit, I remember there was a dinner at the Spanish Embassy, attended by the president of the republic and his wife, the foreign secretary, the secretary of health, the president of the Red Cross, la Bruja, and myself. The queen told us that if we were going to Spain, to let her know through the embassy, I don't know, maybe to entertain us there or something.

I want to tell one more story about the Spanish monarchs. One time they visited the archaeological site at Cacaxtla, and my wife Gabriela and I accompanied them. After the tour, they got on a bus that was to take them back to Mexico City. Queen Sofía realized that she had not told us goodbye. She stopped the bus and got off to say goodbye to us. That's how she is—a great lady.

To sum up, I believe the Templo Mayor at that time had an effect on the famous, as well as the people, who could participate in the discovery of the principal Aztec temple at the same time as the archaeologists. Now let's turn to another aspect, the academic aspect. We might sum it up by saying that specialists on the Aztecs watched these excavations with great interest. So much so, (and they have said this, not I, the opinions of various scholars are well documented) that after these discoveries, the field of Aztec studies was altered. There was a renewed interest in looking more profoundly at what was known about the Aztecs in the light of this new research, the new data. This has resulted in the publication of more than 350 new bibliographical entries by different specialists dealing with the Templo Mayor. You will find studies by Jacques Soustelle, Alfredo López Austin, Miguel León-Portilla, Henry Nicholson, Davíd Carrasco, Tony Aveni, Johanna Broda, Doris Heyden, Michael Graulich, Leonardo López Luján, Felipe Solís, in short, all the great specialists on the Mexica. I believe the Templo Mayor gave them a pattern that allowed them to revise, to make a contribution with their research. And this has had worldwide repercussions.

But, of course, along with this there has been some envy. I mean, colleagues, above all local ones who would like to find fault with what was being done, unfounded criticisms. There were those who criticized but had never come to see the excavations. As I said then, "Well, if they want to criticize, let them come, let them visit and then express an opinion, positive or negative." But they didn't even come, but just went around talking. That reminds me of a story that Cervantes gives us in the *Quijote*. Don Quijote is traveling with Sancho Panza and as they near a town the dogs come out barking furiously. Sancho says to Don Quijote, "Don Quijote, they are going to attack us. The dogs are barking at us." And Don Quijote says, "Yes, Sancho, we are moving, that's why they are barking at us." I mean, people who don't move in their lives, who don't make progress, who don't make a contribution, who don't do anything, well, nobody is going to say anything. They won't be criticized. On the other hand, if you try to do something, and this has particular repercussions. . . .

D: Eduardo, I would like to know if you could pinpoint some interesting, special moments during the excavation when things were found that were important for their impact on our understanding of the Aztec world and the meaning of the Templo Mayor. I know that a great number of things were unearthed, between 7,000 and 8,000 artifacts, but were there some that had a greater impact on our idea of the Aztec world?

E: A lot of discoveries were made during the phase of excavation. In archaeology, the importance of a discovery depends on its context and the information it yields. So, it can happen that sometimes the discovery of a small artifact, for example, may be more important, because of the context it is found in, than an entire building.

I mean, it is all relative and it depends a lot on contextual information. Here, in the case of the Templo Mayor, the over one hundred buried offerings were very important. That is, the large number of offerings, their location, the internal relation between them, the distribution of the objects within each offering. I think in general this is one of the most important elements contained in the Templo Mayor. And why? Because these offerings, as I said, had a language. They were not objects tossed at random into a cist. Instead they were arranged in the offering box, the cist, with absolute premeditation. That means an object was put in a particular place because it had to be in that place according to its symbolic function; we realized the offering is a true microcosm.

The study of the offerings is fundamental for understanding the unique significance of the Templo Mayor. I didn't want to begin an integrative study of the buried offerings until I had very clearly established who would be the right person to carry out this synthetic kind of research. I could see that it would require a person who united several traits. It had to be a person who knew the Templo Mayor, who had been there and observed and participated in the excavation of the offerings so as to have an idea of what the contexts were. It had to be a person who could handle modern computational techniques because the use of these technical means would be indispensable in correlating the huge quantity of information and trying to decipher the language of these offerings. Besides this, it had to be a person who had a profound and extensive understanding of the Mexica world. There was one person who met all three requirements: Leonardo López Luján. He had worked with us, he knew the Mexica world, and he could apply the technology this work required. So he was selected to handle the analysis of the offerings. I believe he has done a truly excellent job.

Studies are now being published by biologists, physical anthropologists, archaeologists, and other specialists. So, these offerings have made this interdisciplinary collaboration possible. I think the results that are coming out now are very important to our understanding of the world of the Mexica. Another discovery had to do with the architectonic and chronological characteristics of the Templo Mayor. Up to the time of the massive excavation, we didn't know about the different superpositions of the building. We only had certain information from written sources about this, but no archaeological data. As we penetrated deeper into the layers of the temple, we had the great good fortune to find the earliest temple almost complete, what we called stage II. That is, we even found the remains of the *adoratorios* or shrines in the upper section with all their elements; the mural paintings, the remains of some associated sculptures, like the *chac mool* on the Tláloc side of the temple, the sacrificial altar on the side of Huitzilopochtli. In short, a tremendous amount of cultural information that told us what the upper part of the temple was like. And then, in later stages we were also able to find significant parts of the lower sections of the temple. That is, the great platform and also its characteristics: the great serpent heads, the altar of the frogs, Coyolxauhqui, the rooms at both ends of the platform which supports the temple. In short, there were some really interesting discoveries about the architecture and sculpture of the Templo Mayor.

On the other hand, there were discoveries like the House of Eagles, which gave us wonderful information about what ritual spaces were like, with large sculptures of warriors and skeletons. We could say that in general all these contextual discoveries were an absolute treasure. Now of course we can look at these discoveries from other perspectives. For example, from an aesthetic point of view. If you ask me, "Aesthetically, what would you consider the most outstanding objects found here?" I would say that the sculpture of Coyolxauhqui is an exceptional aesthetic artifact. It is one of the great Mexica sculptures which we can now add to a great trinity of previously excavated superb sculptures, namely the Coatlicue, the Coyolxauhqui, and the Piedra del Sol. The Piedra del Sol, like the Coatlicue, is a grand recapitulation of the thought and cosmology of the Aztec world. And there are other pieces like the monumental caracol, which we discovered. Sculpturally, the caracol is a marvelous achievement.

I could point out others. Now, if you asked me, for example, what emotion did you feel while you were excavating? Well, in that sense of course, an archaeologist has to be a little cold at the time when he is excavating. He must move ahead very carefully, but that doesn't keep you from feeling some strong emotions when you see or discover something.

I remember the impact I felt when we found offering number 41. It was a stone box with a lid that had the face of Tláloc, and the lid was broken. So we were cleaning the outside of it, taking photographs, collecting all the data, and we were going to take off half of the cover because it was broken. We were surrounded by journalists since we had invited them to watch this. When we removed the top, I saw water. There was water inside, and a face that was looking at me through the water. I mean, a face that was observing me. The sensation was tremendous, the journalists were also saying " Water, water, and there's a face!" And it turned out that the face was a great Mezcala mask and the water had filtered in during the rainy season. Of course there were journalists who wrote, "Matos Finds Five-Hundred-Year-Old Water!" But no, it wasn't five hundred years old, it was just water from the last rainy season. In short, I could tell you that emotions coexisted with scientific interest in learning more about the Mexica world on a daily basis.

The fourth breaking point: the superfluous

D: We've explored the duality of breaking points and liberation in your life and career, in which we note that each great breaking point brings a moment of liberation with it. This seems to be an important pattern in your consciousness. We have talked about the third breaking point, and now it's time to hear about the fourth.

E: I would say that I have lived dialectically, with both quantitative and qualitative interior changes. Each qualitative change has led precisely to that: to a breaking point and something new in my life. Indeed we have discussed my first breaking point, the break with religion, and the second, the break with the power structure of my discipline, the third, the break with my family . . . very painful, but necessary for me to find my own center. Later the Templo Mayor became the center that stabilized me and gave me an absolute security in everything. I rediscovered myself as I was making discoveries in the temple. And then we come to the fourth breaking point. In truth this break is still going on, although I hope to pass through it with that same spirit of willpower. I know that there are superfluous things in our lives, certain external things that people desire. I see it the other way round, that the important things in life are internal, forces that you project so that you see the external world in a different light. As long as a man doesn't lose the ability to appreciate an afternoon or a small leaf falling in an autumn afternoon, he remains human. If he loses this capacity and worries about whether he is going to have a better car, or whether he must be well dressed, if he wants people to notice him because he looks successful, then he loses what makes him a human being. That's what the fourth breaking point is about. Even as my fame has increased, I continue to achieve a greater inner separation from desiring those things, material things that are very attractive. Let me make this clear: I can have a good car, or have a magnificent house and enjoy it. But it is not indispensable. There is a great difference, for example, between dedicating your life to trying to have all kinds of material wealth and status and living your life normally. The key for me is to have a purpose in life that is not focused on fame and wealth. A good example of this disinterest was the time when I left that enormous house and went to live in a small apartment.

I didn't seek out fame. I mean, fame came to me from outside. I accepted it, I enjoyed it, I lived with it, but it is something I don't worry about. Fame is a fickle lady who, when you seek her, hides from you, and may turn up when you ignore her . . .

I think a lot of my companions believe that I love to be on television so I can be seen. But no, I love to be on television so I can explain what archaeology is, or what the Mexica world was like to an enormous number of people who want to know about it. I think the fourth breaking point consists in moving farther and farther away from the superfluous things in life. Now, you don't have to be a monk to do that, you don't have to enter a monastery. You can't avoid being in the world. But, you can achieve an inner peace so that you are not preoccupied with having power, or having the newest car. If I am able to consolidate this break, it will be a fundamental step because I will have broken with the superficial aspects of life. I will be entering into more profound aspects, deeper thinking, learning important secrets.

D: I have had numerous opportunities of visiting your home, and I have always had the impression that you have always lived in a modest apartment, not in a large house. Can you comment on your domestic world, as a reflection of the thoughts you were just expressing?

E: This apartment I lived in during the years of the excavation was part of my interior world. So it mirrored what was in that world. You would be able to see paintings that deal with death, which is a theme that has always fascinated me, and which is certainly connected with the fifth breaking point. . . . You would also see time there. . . . There were lots of clocks, clocks that chimed, these clocks signify time. Remember that the archaeologist is a seeker of lost time. Just as Proust said, "in search of lost time." That's what an archaeologist is, he is searching for the past. So those clocks symbolized time. That implies time lost and time recovered. I mean, it goes toward the past and also toward the future. You would also see very good wine, my pipes, small objects of popular culture, and so on, but you would never see an archaeological artifact. And books, of course. Some colleagues who visited in those years were surprised at not seeing a lot of books about archaeology. Well, yes, I did have archaeology books, of course, but you would find a good number of books on art, books of poetry and literature, and so on, most of which had been read; they were not decorative. You would also see photos of Rilke, Rodin, and the like. All of this made a world that had meaning. I loved to be there inside it. I became more and more sedentary, and I loved to be there with my pipe, reading and writing. There were a lot of candles. In the living room and the dining room, anyway, there were seventeen candles. This also had a meaning, it was all symbolic. I lived there amid lots of symbols. Maybe that reminds you of Mircea Eliade, with respect to the symbols. I mean, I loved to be there. I lived a good part of my life there. Practically every afternoon and of course at night,

I was there. Always accompanied by music as well, generally classical music which served as a background to all this. The music floated among the candles and the pictures and the skeletons there as a part of the whole. And of course la Bruja was there. I mean, María Luisa was there, too. Since she was a witch, she was in the walls, in the pictures, in the mirrors, she was everywhere. It was all part of that interior world.

D: It seems like this description you've given me is of the atelier, but also the blossoming of the atelier. At that time, your apartment with la Bruja was the blossoming of that period of your life.

E: In fact, the atelier was our place. It was our hideout. We painted a huge centaur with my face on one wall there and la Bruja nude with very long hair. Her hair began to tumble down and we painted it in the whole room, I mean, the hair filled the whole room. We had to leave this mural there, and we made a ritual of covering it whenever we left the atelier. La Bruja and I would take a day to cover it so that nobody could see it or desecrate it. But, you are right, inside our apartment we shaped our daily lives as our new atelier with all of our belongings. Everything was in plain sight, visible.

D: When I had the opportunity of coming to dinner with the two of you at your apartment, I noticed a painting of you on the wall. It has the shape of your body . . . while the head has several levels. Can you tell me the story of that painting?

E: Yes, a friend of mine who is a painter did that for me. As you know, I have a lot of good friends who are painters, sculptors, writers and so on. So, a friend who is a painter, Carmen Parra, took a notion one day to paint me. I went to her house and sat. I posed, and she painted me. She made three large canvases. One is in color, and another is just the sketch. And then the one that you saw. In fact part of the head is out of phase, at a different level. And the body is too. She said it represented the mutilation of Coyolxauhqui. She was going to paint me in the various pieces in which the goddess was mutilated. She also made me three drawings in the temple, which I have here, in which you see my head and behind it the Cathedral or parts of the Templo Mayor. She did those while we were excavating. Later we produced a very handsome book with my texts and her serigraphs. It is a bibliographical jewel. Not for the contents, but because there were only one hundred printed copies, all numbered, and because it's beautifully bound.

D: I think you have an impressive head, and a lot of artists would like to use you as a model. What comments have you heard about your fabulous head? Because when the time comes to talk about skulls. . . .

E: Because I am bald, my head is very round. Besides, I wore a large, very long beard. I guess that gave me a very striking appearance. I remember one time here in the Temple, while I was guiding a group, at the end a man came up and told me: "Look, I'm a photographer. I have a photography studio. I'd like to invite you there, because I'd like to do a study of your head."

He gave me his card. Really, a number of photographers have taken my picture because of my head.

I have one, for example, by Flor Garduño, and she is an internationally known photographer. I have a fantastic photograph of myself with the caracol taken by Daisy Asher, also internationally known. That photo by Daisy Asher is impressive: how she captured the movement of the caracol in relation to the movement of my head, my pipe, and my beard. She didn't pose me, she just said: "Stand next to the caracol, and I'll shoot some photos."

And she walked around taking photos, and one came out that I really liked. It's been published in a book of one hundred Mexican personalities. Of course Daisy is a great photographer, and it really shows here. Once she told me that the two photos she liked best were of Tamayo and me.

D: Speaking of your humble but fabulous apartment of those years. I often remember the idea of Eliade, that the sacred is often hidden in the most everyday places. In your description of your apartment, it sounds like it was the sacred space of a fabulous imagination. Perhaps one of the most important results of this sacred space was the birth of your new son, Rainer María. I would like to hear about your experience since he came into the world, and what impact that has had on your new life.

E: La Bruja always wanted to have a child, but she had problems; very serious problems because she couldn't carry a child to term, she miscarried, and she felt very despondent, very frustrated. I remember when I went to teach a course in France in 1983, she was pregnant. Then we visited the tomb of Rilke, we made the trip through Spain, and arrived in France to teach the course. She started to have trouble there. The French doctor who treated her recommended that she return to Mexico, that the airplane would not cause a problem, and that she should go back to Mexico to rest. I stayed and taught the course in the École des Hautes Études in Paris, and she went back to Mexico. But she miscarried again. She was very unhappy, but always maintained her hope and determination to have a child.

We always talked about what we would name our child. There was no doubt: if it was a boy, he would be named Rainer María, like Rilke. If it was a girl, she would have the names of witches. So we had about seven names: Morgana, Estebania, Camila, Federica, and so on, a lot of names, and at one time we planned to give her all of them. Fortunately, it was a boy. So we just named him Rainer María.

D: But his birth was also complicated because of the date, right? Remember, we had made plans then for you to come to Boulder to lead a seminar.

E: That's right. We were looking at the dates, and kept thinking there might be some problem, that it might be moved forward or back, and so on, because of all that had happened before. Finally, Rainer was born on November 11, 1989. It was very important because he came to shape the world we lived in. When he was a year and a few months old he was a child with a free spirit and we wanted to cultivate that sense of freedom in him. You could tell he was a very intelligent boy. We wanted him to be some sort of artist, a musician or poet, but knew he would eventually choose his own path. From the time he was in his mother's womb, la Bruja put classical music on and put the earphones on her belly so he could hear that music. His mere presence was very important. And for María Luisa it was a great accomplishment in her life.

D: Speaking of classical music, do you have any favorite pieces?

E: I must confess, I liked to have the whole apartment filled with classical music. Filling all that microcosm of mine and la Bruja's and filling us as well. Our favored composers ranged from Beethoven to Bach, Vivaldi, Hayden, etc. Really the selection of music depends on one's mood. I sometimes like to hear Falla or Albéniz . . . Spaniards, or sometimes I want to hear opera or Baroque music. Another thing we liked a lot were the Gregorian chants for nuns which were composed by Hildegard in Germany, around the twelfth or thirteenth century, very ancient, which have been rediscovered. We had a record, which we found very deeply moving the first time we heard it. That was at the home of Juan José Bremer, who was the Ambassador to Washington many years later. It made a real impression. We started to look for the record. We could not find it anywhere until a friend who was French, an Air France pilot, got it for us. From that day on, the songs of the abbess Hildegard were played often in our home. This doesn't mean we didn't like popular music, of course. We did listen to it. It all depended on the moment and the mood.

From interdisciplinary research to the "Erectario" and *Turandot*

L: What is the importance of teamwork to you?

E: As far as collective, interdisciplinary work, I have always thought it should be done that way. And really, Mexican anthropology was born of an interdisciplinary, multidisciplinary team as evidenced by the work of Don Manuel Gamio in Teotihuacan. When I met Davíd Carrasco we started talking a lot about this. He was a scholar of religious history at the University of Colorado in Boulder. I talked to him about the importance of establishing meetings with different specialists and creating an archive which he named the Moses Mesoamerican Archive. That's how we agreed to have the first meeting in Boulder, and Davíd undertook to get the necessary funding. There were people like Pedro Armillas, Johanna Broda, Doris Heyden, Alfredo López Austin, Paul Wheatley, Henry Nicholson, John Hoag, and others, people dedicated to diverse aspects of understanding the past. As you can see, there were archaeologists, historians, specialists in religions, in art, in short, truly interdisciplinary, wouldn't you say? This allowed a very rich interchange among all of us.

From Colorado it moved to Princeton and from there to Harvard, where Davíd augmented the archive with slides, articles, and so on. The publications of these meetings were the first priority; we had a meeting and we published. I don't know how many meetings we have had by now, but each of them has its respective publication. It was interesting to observe how the thinking of some of us changed over time, and also how the membership changed since new people came in who were working and forming their own opinions. The original idea was to alternate the meetings between the United States and Mexico.

L: To return to the subject of interdisciplinary studies, I have a question about Manuel Gamio. In a number of forums and publications you have insisted on the applicability of the model of Manuel Gamio at Teotihuacan in the twenty-first century, with a global, interdisciplinary vision. My question is this: looking to the future, how would you complement this model? And where do you think this model would be most productive?

E: For many years we have said that an investigation cannot be done from the perspective of a single discipline. So then, we have talked about interdisciplinary, multidisciplinary, transdisciplinary approaches; Emmanuel Wallerstein, to complicate things even more, has spoken of a unidisciplinary approach. Don Manuel Gamio applied an integrated focus in Teotihuacan in 1917 which was based on two categories: population and territory, seen in an integral way, studying Pre-hispanic, Colonial, and Modern periods, by using a group of scholars from different fields of knowledge. So you can see that anthropology in Mexico was born from an interdisciplinary and multidisciplinary focus. He considered anthropology to be made up of such disciplines as archaeology, ethnology, physical anthropology, and linguistics, as well as sciences such as geology, mineralogy, and others. From that perspective, we can see that he was a visionary, a pioneer who tried in his studies to define a set of problems and solve them on the basis of the research done by diverse sciences. And what is more important: all his work is directed toward improving the lives of the present population.

I always recommend that my students read *La población del Valle de Teotihuacán* so they will be familiar with the principles Gamio started with. Even though the study may contain some errors, there is no doubt that in broad outline it is impressive. Maybe by reading it the students can understand why we study the various anthropological disciplines in ENAH, and how they can help to better the population being studied. Gamio's study gained him international recognition for considering anthropology to be a science with a practical purpose.

So now, what validity does this have in today's world? Clearly scientific research has become progressively more diversified. We have super-specialization but at the same time we recognize the necessity of turning to other sciences to complement the data. This led José Luis Lorenzo to create the Laboratorios de Prehistoria around 1961. Different specialists like geologists, paleontologists, biologists, chemists, and others collaborate there. This was a great step forward for archaeology. I also agree that certain research can be undertaken by archaeology alone, depending on the subject, but the wealth of data that is obtained by bringing in other disciplines allows the accumulation of much more information. From this perspective, I think that Gamio was the first to apply this idea. Of course it should be clear that we are not talking about applying Gamio's model just the way he conceived of it in his day. The social sciences and history have improved a great deal both in theory and in practice, so that one has to incorporate a totally new technology into one's research.

Where could an integral research method with these characteristics be applied? At times I have thought, "If I were named director of INAH, I would invite my colleagues from the various branches of anthropology to choose three or four regions in which to do integral studies, and simultaneously invite economists, sociologists, architects, geologists, chemists, and others who might be needed to join the projects." The central valleys of Oaxaca, which have had an enormous human potential from the Pre-hispanic period right up to the present, might be one of these regions. The Tarascan region, with its ancient, colonial, and modern wealth, might be another. Veracruz and the Mayan region might be yet another. In this way, we could make a comparison among these regions in their different periods and assess their social and economic possibilities for the future.

The idea is there. I was never director of the INAH at a time when this sort of research was feasible. When the directorship was offered to me in 2000 the time was not right. I believe that everything has its time, and the time for me to be director had already passed.

D: This idea of multidisciplinary work is also reflected in your youth, isn't it? Your spiritualism, your materialism, and the aspect of art. We know that you are a sculptor, that you acted in a Mexican movie called *Tequila,* that you were in an opera, and that you choreographed a ballet called *Mictlan Nueve.* You have also written poetry like the "Erectario." In a sense all of this is multidisciplinary.

E: From my early youth onward I have felt a strong attraction to art. If I had been asked what I wanted to be, I would have answered archaeologist, novelist, or poet. I have tried writing some. I have also tried to paint. I went into a free workshop at the Academia de San Carlos with Edmundo Aquino and started painting. Fortunately, I have a good sense of self-criticism and when I looked at my paintings I said, "These are awful. I am sorry, but this is not it. Clearly." I also wrote poetry. The best of it is the "Erectario," which deals with those erotic thoughts which I feel can be expressed without falling into the scatological. It is about the sexual relations between a centaur and his mate. It manages to describe the 69 in a way that leaves no doubt, but is still rather subtle:

We have formed a perfect communicant vessel:
You feed me on your essence of woman,
As I spill into your mouth
The life that escapes me fleeting . . .

So, in a few words, in a simple way, it expresses a marvelous, common act of love, right? Once I published some five or six poems from the "Erectario" in the cultural supplement *Sábado*, which was directed by my good friend the journalist Fernando Benítez. An interesting thing happened. We were at the award ceremony for a sculpture competition which Teresa del Conde had asked me to help judge, when a young woman came up to me and said: "Excuse me. Are you Eduardo Matos?"

"Yes, I am."

"Ah. Well, look. I wanted to tell you that I read your poems from the 'Erectario' in *Sábado*, and we liked them so well that my husband and I cut them out and put them on the closet door. And let me tell you we were so inspired by them, that I now have a son."

I was stunned. I thought, "'Erectario' was good for something after all . . ."

I have continued to publish. It has even been said that there is trace of the poetic in my archaeological writing. Could be. Whenever I write there is always musical accompaniment although I have never tried to compose melodies, because I don't understand musical notation. I would rather listen than create a mess like I did with the painting. I have always had such an interest in art that I told the directors of Bellas Artes, who were friends of mine: Listen, sometime let me participate. Maybe in an opera as part of the cast of extras or in an orchestra where I just play the triangle.

An opportunity came up soon. One day in 1977 the director of International Relations of Bellas Artes, Luis del Valle Prieto, called and said: "Listen, do you seriously want to participate in an opera?"

"Of course. Why?"

"Because we are staging *Turandot* and we thought of having you play the Persian Prince. If you are interested, come now and rehearse."

I didn't think twice. I left my office at the Council of Archaeology and went straight to the Palacio de Bellas Artes. The rehearsal was over when I got there but I went up to the director Pepe Solé who told me: "They told me you were coming. You are going to play the Persian Prince who enters at the beginning of the opera. Your beard is ideal for the part."

"All right. What do I have to do?"

"Look. It's very simple. Your part is in the first act of the opera. You are up there above the stage, and you enter, walking between guards, come down fourteen steps, and you ask the Princess Turandot for clemency. She refuses, and then you walk slowly, but very proudly—remember you are a prince—and you go with the guards to be decapitated."

"Good. It sounds easy."

"Let's see. Go up and make your entrance."

So I did. I walked slowly and came to the place where I had to come down the fourteen steps. I did that. When I got down he told me: "Now, turn toward where Turandot is and you lift your left arm to ask her pardon. Very good. Now you exit very proudly between the four guards who are taking you to be decapitated, and that's all. Run through that a few times, and then go up to the offices and pick out your prince costume."

I went through it several times by myself and finally convinced myself that what I had to do was very simple. I went up to wardrobe and selected a suit covered in pearls, but I told the person in charge: "Listen. Get me a prince's hat, but one that covers my face a bit, because if Don Gastón García Cantú, the director of the INAH, sees me looking like this, he'll fire me from the institution."

Once I was measured and all I asked the person in charge: "Listen. When is the opera? When do we rehearse again?"

"This was the last rehearsal. The opera begins this Friday. Come two hours before 8:00 so we can do your makeup."

I should make clear that it was Wednesday so it was just two days away. I was terrified that my debut was so soon. But I was committed so I showed up on Friday and after my makeup I went off to find my costume and then looked for my dressing room to change. *Turandot* is an opera that requires a lot of actors, so I saw an immense number of people going by dressed as Chinese. I asked one of them: "Excuse me. Do you know where my dressing room is?"

"What role do you play?"

"Well, the Persian Prince. . . ."

"Oh man! What dressing room? No, go in that room there and change."

After that humiliation of the Persian Prince, I went to the room where there were about fifty people changing and dressing like Chinese. I prudently stayed close to the wall, and transformed myself into the Persian Prince. I left and the show was about to start, so I went and climbed up to where I was supposed to be. There was a young man there who gave the actors their cues to enter on stage. He said: "Stand right here. The first one who goes on is the guy who has the sword they're going to behead you with; then you go out, and then the guards. I'll tell you when."

I took a deep breath and kept thinking, "What the hell am I doing here, what was I thinking?" The opera started and the fellow with the sword started walking. He turned to me and indicated that I should go on stage, too.

"Now! Start walking."

Just as I started to take the first step, a guy who was backstage started making signs at me. I didn't understand what he wanted to tell me, and he signaled "glasses." I had forgotten to take off my glasses! In the meantime, the kid who was giving the orders was urging me: "Move! Get on stage!"

I didn't know what to do. I took off my glasses and had nowhere to put them except in the sleeve of my costume. I started forward behind the actor with the sword, who by this time had already gone quite a distance. I reached the place where I was to go down the steps and it turned out the lights were in my eyes. I couldn't locate the first step because I couldn't see a thing. I began to feel around with my foot until I found the edge of the step. I began to descend slowly—yes in a very noble manner—and then I noticed a large group of Chinese who were harassing me, something I didn't expect since I hadn't rehearsed with the whole cast. Just then, the guards who are in charge of me started in on me: "Come on, Gramps, step on it!"

"Hey, guys! Don't screw me up!"

I descended the stairs and arrived at the bottom. I turned to look at Turandot and lifted my left arm to plead for clemency. My glasses, which were in my left sleeve, slid down inside and came to rest at my waist. "En la madre," I thought. I finished my part as well as I could and made my exit in as princely a manner as possible. On Sunday I repeated the process, and swore to myself that I would never do it again, not even if they offered me a part in *Nabucco* as a palm tree!

D: So, then, what about the movie?

E: Oh! About *Tequila*. Well, *Tequila* is a film by Gámiz. He is a filmmaker who was very well known years earlier as a very good director. He had withdrawn to make commercial videos, and he was returning to cinema with a screenplay by Carlos Monsiváis. He contacted me and said he wanted me to be in the movie in one particular shot. He asked me to be in the Zócalo at 5:00 in the morning, in front of the Cathedral. My part was to walk forward and stop, crouch down on the floor and nail a board down on it. Then I was to stand up, look around anxiously, and exit. That was my part.

D: And that was here in Mexico?

E: Here, in the Zócalo. I had to repeat the scene like five times, but we finally got it. It was important to me to take part in the return of a great director like Gámiz, and to have even a small part in the film.

D: Excellent. And what can you tell us about the ballet *Mictlan Nueve*?

E: *Mictlan Nueve* was a choreography that I organized with a great ballerina of modern dance to be presented in a theater at the university. The name reflects the fact that the ballet presents the nine steps which the dead go through to arrive at Mictlan, in the Nahua worldview. It is done in one act, and the dancers captured the sense of it very well. It starts with the presence of the god Tlaltecuhtli, who devours the cadavers which then pass through a series of dangers. She and I met with the dancers. I talked to them about the subject. I gave them some readings on the Nahua way of thinking about death, and the steps to Mictlan, the underworld. I think the results were interesting.

Fig 16. Matos assisting in the application of conservation materials on the Coyolxauhqui in the Templo Mayor, 1978.

Fig 17. Excavating "stage II" at the Templo Mayor in 1979.

Fig 18. Excavating an offering at the Templo Mayor in 1979.

Fig 19. Eduardo excavating a sculpture of the Old God, Huehuetéotl, at the Templo Mayor in 1980.

Fig 20. On the occasion of the 1978 visit to the Templo Mayor by the Spanish rulers, Don Juan Carlos and Doña Sofía.

Fig 21. Eduardo Matos giving a tour of the Cacaxtla excavations to the Queen of Spain, Doña Sofía.

Fig 22. With the famous Mexican actress María Félix during her visit to the Templo Mayor in February of 1979.

Fig 23. With the artist José Luis Cuevas at the Templo Mayor, December 27, 1979.

Fig 24. On being appointed as a new member of the National Academy of History and Geography of Mexico.

Fig 25. The president of France, Valéry Giscard D'Estaing, accompanied by Matos's good friend the distinguished Mesoamericanist Jacques Soustelle, March 1, 1979.

Fig 26. Eduardo accompanying the president of France Valéry Giscard D'Estaing and the archaeologist Jacques Soustelle at the Templo Mayor.

Fig 27. Eduardo Matos describes aspects of the excavation to the French President François Miterrand and his wife in 1981.

Fig 28. Giving a lecture at the Getty Institute.

Fig 29. Eduardo Matos, Davíd Carrasco, Doris Heyden, and Xavier Noguez during a Mesoamerican Archive meeting in the Templo Mayor.

Fig 30. Eduardo Matos, José Cuellar, and Davíd Carrasco at the University of Colorado, Boulder, at a summer seminar co-led by Carrasco and Matos.

Fig 31. Meeting at the Mesoamerican Archive at the University of Colorado, Boulder.

Fig 32. With Octavio Paz (center) and his wife Marie Jo at the Templo Mayor excavations on April 8, 1981. Paz later won the Nobel Prize for literature.

Fig 33. Gabriel García Márquez, winner of the Nobel Prize for Literature, visited the Templo Mayor on November 8, 1980.

Fig 34. Eduardo Matos at the Templo Mayor with Rigoberta Menchú, winner of the 1992 Nobel Peace Prize. Rigoberto's Nobel Prize medal and citation are on permanent display in the Templo Mayor Museum in Mexico City.

Fig 35. A caricature of Eduardo Matos with his inseparable pipe.

Fig 36. This cartoon of Matos came out during an oil crisis when the United States showed heightened interest in Mexican oil. Matos is shown excavating the Templo Mayor and discovering, not petroleum but "black waters."

Fig 37. As a sign of Matos's growing fame, he was depicted in a series of newspaper cartoons and caricatures. From the cover of the magazine *Siempre* we see Matos holding up a Rain God (Tláloc) urn while the general director of INAH, Gastón García Cantú, looks on.

Fig 38. This caricature of Matos says "I want to put at your disposal my new discovery: this stone for ritual sacrifices to the war god Huitzilopochtli." This appeared during the presidential elections in Mexico.

Fig 39. A caricature of President Jimmy Carter dressed as a Mexican charro (cowboy) during his visit to the Templo Mayor excavations.

Fig 40. Another caricature of Matos saying "And we are going to unearth the past before we bury the present."

Fig 41. Eduardo Matos is well known for his wit and humor as shown in this picture where he and Dr. Dominique Verut pretend to be unemployed arqueologists advertising their skills alongside day laborers who daily line up at this location next to the Cathedral of Mexico.

CHAPTER FIVE

The Aztecs Conquer the World

L: BASED ON THE MUSEUMS YOU HAVE CREATED and the expositions you have organized in Mexico and in other countries, what are your thoughts about museums and popularization?

E: As to museums, my first experience came when I took on the rehabilitation of the small museum in the archaeological zone of Cuicuilco. I saw that it was closed and that it had certain defects. This was about 1969. I invited a good museographer, José Lameiras, to help me. With his assistance it was possible to give a good idea of what that site had been like. We placed burials with their offerings and reopened the museum to the public. Later on my connection with museums was much stronger. I would say it began when I was named director of the Museo Nacional de Antropología, which I felt as a mixed blessing. I'll explain: We are talking about the years from 1983 through 1985, when I was the director of the Centro de Investigaciones y Estudios Superiores en Antropología Social (CIESAS). In 1986 I got a call from the subsecretary of culture telling me that the secretary wanted me to take over the directorship of the Museo Nacional de Antropología. You have to keep in mind that just a few months before this, in December of 1985, there was a burglary at that museum. Changes needed to be made in the security systems of the museum and the secretary thought I was the right person to oversee them.

They made me the offer, and on one hand I felt quite proud because the museum is the institution that made the beginnings of Mexican archaeology possible; the great scholars of the nineteenth century were concentrated there and it had a tremendous history.

On the other hand, I felt sad because CIESAS was a research center which, despite its small size, generated studies of a very high quality and I was able to implement certain ideas and plans. But I accepted and went to Chapultepec. Since the offer came directly from the secretary of education, and the museo is under INAH, I was worried about how its director, Enrique Florescano, would be notified of the change. I have never liked to play power politics and although I was not on good terms with Florescano I mentioned my concern to the subsecretary. He told me that he had asked for three names from which to select the director of the museum, and Florescano had given them to him. My name was not among them. The subsecretary had told him: "Listen, nobody knows who these three people are. What would you think of Eduardo Matos?"

He answered: "Oh, of course! Matos was the fourth name on my list."

I don't know if this was true, but that's what I was told. The result was that I assumed the directorship of the museum and we immediately began to look at what could be done. I first did a complete study of all the rooms, from which I concluded that they were a little out of date as far as the information they contained. So I decided to change them. I started with the Sala de Orígenes, or the populating of America and its prehistory. This coincided with a conference that we organized with the support of the secretary of public education, on the populating of the continent. We were advised by José Luis Lorenzo, who was reluctant because he felt a bit out of the loop. I presented an outline that introduced the ideas of Childe about the Neolithic Revolution, that is, the moment when humans discovered agriculture and took a qualitative step forward in the process of development. We used the findings of Richard MacNeish's studies in Puebla, Tamaulipas, and Chiapas, in which he determined the age of such cultivated plants as corn, squash, beans, avocado, and others. We also incorporated skulls from the Texcal Cave in Puebla from the same period. It was also important to include the artifacts found in association with the mammoth from Santa Isabel Ixtapa, the only discovery that allowed us to make the association of man with megafauna. The idea was to keep updating the rooms, introducing the newest archaeological findings. I was not able to continue because I was only director of the museum for a year and two months. The work was later carried on by Mari Carmen Serra, and has been continued by Felipe Solís.

After that, I had the experience of the Museum of the Templo Mayor. From the beginning of the excavations in 1978, I proposed the necessity of having an on-site museum that would show what the building was and also some aspects of Aztec society. The plan of exhibits was designed to give an idea of both the economic elements and the religious superstructure present in the Templo Mayor. To that end, we had an arrangement of eight rooms, divided into two wings. The first room presented a history of the discoveries of Aztec sites over the centuries. The second and third rooms showed the expansion of the Aztec into other regions with the resulting tributes levied on the conquered groups, as evidenced by the materials found in the excavation. The fourth room, which occupied the highest level of the museum, showed the gods associated with war. From there one passed into another room with the gods associated with water, and then down to an impressive room showing the flora and fauna, which was done by the biologist Óscar Polaco. From there one went on into the room of agriculture, the calendar, and the market. The final room dealt with the colonial and modern periods. As you can see, the lower rooms held those things that related to history and economic structure, while the upper rooms showed the religion, with the gods of war and death on one hand and the gifts of the gods related to agricultural production on the other. It was a way of demonstrating the relation between the structure and the superstructure.

A traveling exhibit of the discoveries from the Templo Mayor was also set up and traveled to a number of cities in Mexico. I don't know if it is still being done, but it was very well received by the public in the cities where it was presented.

The last archaeological museum I was involved in was the one in Teotihuacan. You have to remember that the first museum on this site was set up by Don Leopoldo Batres in the first decade of the twentieth century. It was located south of the Pyramid of the Sun. In the sixties it was relocated across from the Ciudadela, in a rather unfortunate building that doesn't allow the visitor to see the external part of the Ciudadela complex. They had considered knocking it down or installing a video which would allow the visitor to orient himself. We wanted to locate the new museum on a geographical site that had already been disrupted by previous construction. So we decided to place it on the same site where Batres had built his. That is, an area that was already affected by construction but was very discreet. The building wouldn't be visible from the nearby sites. The new museum was 29 meters by 36 meters, and was designed by Pedro Ramírez Vázquez. The exhibits, which I designed, show the environment and such different aspects of daily life as the growth of the city, the economy, the social classes, and the products of the artisans in the eastern wing. From there one goes to a central model of part of the city, and in the background, through a huge window, one sees the Pyramid of the Sun. Continuing into the western wing one sees the world of the dead and the forms of burials, with a reproduction of the burials in the Temple of Quetzalcóatl and others. This leads into the section of art and the gods. And then on into the relations with other contemporaneous groups.

International exhibits: from Paris to Denver and other cities . . .

E: The expositions outside the country gave me an understanding, an experience with handling the artifacts from packing and shipping to exhibiting. One of the most impressive was the exposition on the

Templo Mayor at the Petit Palais as part of a tour that began in Paris and passed through various countries to end in New York. I remember that the excavations of the Templo Mayor were known worldwide, which had created an enormous interest in seeing the artifacts. This exposition was inaugurated by four ministers, two French and two Mexican.

D: When was this?

E: This was in 1981 and the museographer was Mario Vázquez. Another policy that I established for any exposition on the Templo Mayor, however small it might be, whether in the country or out, was that it should always be accompanied by a conservator. I learned this from an exhibition of Goya that came to Bellas Artes and had a conservator in charge. It was indispensable to have someone to monitor the condition of the pieces. To get back to Paris, the exposition was very successful. The catalog sold well, it had good publicity, and that's how things went in the other European countries all the way through to the American Museum of Natural History in New York. Other exhibitions were presented in Rimini, Italy and some pieces from the Templo Mayor were included in the show "Esplendor de 30 Siglos" presented in the Metropolitan Museum of New York, in San Antonio, and in Los Angeles.

In 1992 there was an exhibition in Madrid coordinated by three scholars: Dr. Miguel León-Portilla, José Alcina Franch, and myself. It was on the occasion of the encounter between the two worlds of Europe and Mesoamerica, which some call the "Discovery of America." A good number of specialists collaborated on the catalog, which was entitled *Azteca-Mexica*. These catalogs have become genuine compendia of studies that bring the reader up to date on the society being studied. Later, in 2003, an exhibition was presented in Santillana del Mar, Spain, with the theme "Iberoamérica Mestiza" in which I collaborated with Dr. León-Portilla. It was also presented in the Castillo de Chapultepec the following year.

The last exhibition that Felipe Solís and I coordinated was in London, organized by the Royal Academy of Arts. It dealt with the Aztecs. The site was in Picadilly very near the location of the Egyptian Hall where the first exposition on ancient and contemporary Mexico was presented in 1824. That was done by William Bullock with the support of the Mexican government. But to get back to our exhibition, it had a specific focus: to show an integrated picture of Aztec society, along with its antecedents, the Teotihuacanos and the Toltecs. One of our successes was bringing together around twenty manuscripts, something it would be very difficult to do again in the future.

That exhibition had phenomenal success. Close to a half million people went to see it. In fact, some young Mexicans made a video in which they interviewed the visitors. It is interesting to hear the opinion of an English child of about eleven years who was asked if he liked the exhibit, if it hadn't been a bit bloody. The child answered to this effect: "Well, every people on earth has its bloody aspects, its wars, its massacres. We see that in the history of England. In truth, the part I liked the best was the Eagle Warriors."

From the interviews done, we found that the part that attracted the most attention was indeed the Eagle Warriors. This vindicates the thinking of Miguel Gamio, when in the early decades of the twentieth century he collected a group of educated people, who had some understanding of the pre-hispanic world, and placed a group of ancient artifacts in front of them and asked them: "Which of these articles do you think we could consider works of art?"

They separated the pieces into two groups: the ones that they thought were works of art, and the ones that they judged not to be. Gamio concluded that these judgments betrayed a psychological bias, since the pieces considered objects of art all reminded one somehow of Greco-Roman art. By contrast, those not considered art were those that had no trace of similarity to remind the viewer of Occidental art.

This exhibit moved on later to Berlin, Bonn, and Rome, and was then installed in the Guggenheim in New York. From there it will go to the Guggenheim in Bilbao. It is expected that more than a million people will visit it.

To finish this subject of museums I want to mention one thing. I have always thought that in Mexico the museums are a form of ideological control. What I mean is that it's not about just going to the museum to see and enjoy the exhibits, as happens in many European museums which have appropriated pieces over long periods of time from Egyptian, Sumerian, Greek, Roman, and other cultures. Instead, it's about appreciating the different societies of ancient Mexico and we have to feel an attachment to that reality. We are observing a part of our history. I have always criticized the Museo de Antropología because it is not a museum of pre-hispanic art, since it doesn't handle the concepts of art. But neither is it a museum of anthropology because it doesn't present a clear picture of those societies. It has always been something of a hybrid, despite the fact that it is a magnificent museum. That is why in the Templo Mayor I tried to show the Aztec culture in an integrated way, and examine such aspects as human sacrifice, which was not shown in the Museo de Antropología. And we gave the subject of warfare, which is barely outlined in the Museo de Antropología, its true level of importance in the Templo Mayor. It wasn't simply a matter of showing the splendid Aztec sculpture, but of showing it in the context of the society that produced it.

L: In that sense, would you agree that in your three museums, Cuicuilco, Teotihuacan, and the Templo Mayor, there is a combination of two crosscurrents: the didactic, teaching museum, which centers on general aspects of anthropology, and the museum of art? Visiting those museums I get the feeling that neither of these types is predominant.

E: Correct. I think it is important to show every aspect of the production of the artifacts as well as the artifacts themselves because this tells us a lot about the society that produced them. From that point of view, really, I try to show both aspects. The museums that show the history of Mexico are very important so they ought to show us our historical reality and not try to hide things that seem negative to us. Historical reality should prevail. The children who visit museums are affected by what they observe, which creates a huge responsibility to show this reality just the way it happened. The museum is an extremely important medium of communication.

LLL: You have not mentioned what may have been your greatest challenge in combining these aesthetic and didactic aspects: the exposition, "Descubridores del pasado en Mesoamérica."

E: One of the three great themes I have analyzed throughout my academic life has been the history of archaeology. In this exhibition I presented a recognition of those who had practiced archaeology, showing the personal effects of some who had already passed on. I think this aspect of the exhibit was effective based on the comments I heard from visitors. On the other hand, it showed the evolution of the discipline, the way it continually developed, along with the objects found by the archaeologists. To do that we decided to combine three elements: the object discovered, the archaeologist who discovered it, and the subsequent publication. That way the visitor could see immediately that the archaeological objects and their contexts are found by specific archaeologists, and how the discoveries are made known by means of publications which are the product of the archaeologist's intellect. These three aspects were very important because they carried the message that people don't go to the museum to see a beautiful or ugly object, that's not so important. What's important is that what they see has a meaning which is communicated by a publication.

The catalog of "Descubridores . . ." shows the evolution of the discipline from its beginnings to the present day. I invited distinguished professionals to supervise the rooms dealing with their specialties, and to contribute the article dealing with their specialties in the catalog. So we had Mari Carmen Serra on the Preclassic period in the Valley; Teotihuacan was under my supervision, as were the introductory room and the Tula room. Xochicalco was in the capable hands of Leonardo López Luján; the Mayas were assigned to Mercedes de la Garza and Agustín Peña; the Olmecs to Beatriz de la Fuente; Veracruz to Rubén Morante; Oaxaca to Nelly Robles; Occidente to Ángeles Olay; the Mexica to Felipe Solís, and the prehistory to Joaquín García Bárcena.

I would like to mention that, like the "Descubridores . . ." shown in the Antiguo Colegio de San Ildefonso, there was also a previous exhibit that I coordinated in the same venue which was called "Dioses del México Antiguo." It was a tremendous success and is still remembered by a lot of people. Miguel León-Portilla, Alfredo López Austin, Felipe Solís, and I wrote articles for the catalog, and I also asked for and included an article by the museographer Miguel Ángel Fernández.

I should add that in general, at the national level as well as internationally, each time that an exhibit is mounted it is accompanied not only by its corresponding catalog, but also by lectures. That was done in France, Italy, Spain, Germany, the United States, and, of course, in Mexico.

D: Many of the interviews I have done with you for this book were done before our exhibition in Denver in 1992–93 which was titled

"Aztecs: the World of Moctezuma." One of the reasons for organizing that exhibition was that Denver, Colorado is part of Aztlán, isn't that right? A lot of Mexican-Americans there were very interested in the exhibition. I'd like to hear your thoughts about "Aztecs: the World of Moctezuma." as one of the organizers of that exhibition, and what is your analysis of what happened there.

E: I do think that the exhibition in Denver was important, precisely because of the place it was shown. In Colorado there is a strong presence of people of Mexican origin who wanted to learn about that history. It was also important to bring a message about the present-day Aztec people and show it through the methods of exhibition. I remember that the exhibition was in the Museum of Natural History and that we faced a very special set of problems. They arose when the local indigenous people came to us to say that, because they respected their indigenous brothers in Mexico, they didn't want the bones of their Aztec ancestors put on display. I remember that we talked about this. I told you that we didn't have this problem in Mexico, since there is a certain pride in prehistoric Mexico. And yet the present-day indigenous population is thought of by some people as a problem, which has created considerable social repercussions. The pre-hispanic indigenous person, who is dead, excites a certain exaltation. Their virtues are greatly appreciated: that they were great architects, artists, and so on . . . while the present-day indigenous person is marginalized. I think this exaltation of the ancient indigenous population comes from the time of Mexico's independence in the early nineteenth century, when there was an effort to find ties to the pre-hispanic past. They attempted to create an image of a strong, unified nation before the conquest, which was then destroyed by Spanish colonialism. Of course that was a false image, since we know that in pre-hispanic Mexico there were great struggles for power, for land, the conquest of one people by another, and so forth.

That's why I was really struck by this problem of the bones. I could see two solutions. I told you, "Tell them that I am going to talk to them as a descendant of Moctezuma, and explain to them that in Mexico there is no problem with the exhibition of human bones." It might well have stopped the whole thing right there. The other solution was simpler: I imagined there would be good reproductions of skulls and bones in plastic or some other material which would not give rise to any problems. That's what we ended up doing.

D: The same problem came up with the first exhibition on Tlatelolco we mounted in Denver, the one entitled "Tlatelolco, dios del viento" (Tlatelolco, Gods of Wind).

E: That's right! The large urns with burials in them discovered at Tlatelolco by Salvador Guilliem Arroyo were exhibited since there were no complete human burials found in the Templo Mayor, except for a few crania. The Tlatelolco exhibit included reproductions of test pits for excavations with those urns and the burials. But in the "Aztecs" exhibit we also used a few crania as part of the offerings. But I think that exhibitions like the ones done in Denver have an ideological purpose, the purpose of explaining Aztec society. Because they do go so far as to exaggerate at times, don't they? You hear such things as "No, no. The Aztecs didn't perform human sacrifices." And why? Because they consider that to be something barbaric. They don't talk about it in terms of the reasoning that motivated human sacrifices. We know that human sacrifice has been practiced by many diverse peoples of the world: Greeks, Romans, the Chinese, and others, especially among agrarian societies. Why? Because this is common to a certain type of society in which it is part of the ritual, mythic expression. Whenever journalists, whether they're Mexican or from another country, ask me about human sacrifice among the Aztecs, I tell them: "Look. Of course there was human sacrifice, but

you need an anthropological understanding of what human sacrifice means. In our age, we sacrificed a hundred thousand people with
one bomb, and for much less plausible reasons. In their past it was a
mythic question; now it's for economic and commercial reasons. I am
better inclined toward those other times."

I think Denver was very important from that perspective.

D: You have had the opportunity to visit museums all over the world:
in China, in Europe, in the United States, and I wonder if you think
the museums here in Mexico, particularly the ones you have been
able to create, are different? Because in Mexico, the majority of the
museums date from the twentieth century, and in Europe they were
built in other centuries. Here they have the spirit of living Mexico. Is
there a difference between Mexican and European museums?

E: Let's start with the contents. The great European museums collected pieces brought from other regions especially in the nineteenth
century, a period of great colonial expansion. They were located in
the palaces or houses of that epoch. They took great pride in exhibiting pieces from Egypt, Mesopotamia, Greece, China, Mexico . . .
That is, foreign societies which were often considered "classical" or
"exotic." By contrast, what we exhibit in Mexico is ours, our history. That is a fundamental difference, isn't it? Here we see our own
essence; there they see the history of others. When Melina Mercuri
was the Secretary of Culture of Greece, she asked the British government to return the friezes from the Parthenon. That created a sort
of coalition among European museums which would not allow even
one object to be returned to its respective country. Why? Because
pieces from those other countries form the core of their museums.
Something similar happened to us with the so-called "Headdress
of Moctezuma," which is in the Ethnographic Museum of Vienna.
Mexico asked for it to be returned and . . . nothing.

L: What else can you tell us about your scholarly activities outside Mexico?

E: I'll start with lectures. So far, I have given close to a thousand, most of them in Mexico, on the theme of the Templo Mayor and the subject of death in the pre-hispanic world. I have spoken in countries on four continents (I'm missing Africa). I had the pleasure of speaking, for example, at the university in Australia that Gordon Childe is associated with. And of course before my speech, we drank some fine wine and toasted that great Australian archaeologist. As to Europe, I have lectured at various times in Spain, France, Italy, Belgium, Germany, and the Soviet Union. In England I spoke at the University of Cambridge, thanks to my friend Colin Renfrew and to Ignacio Durán, who served as the cultural attaché in London. In Asia, I have spoken in India and China. On our continent, in Cuba, Santo Domingo, Puerto Rico, Jamaica, Honduras, Panama, Colombia and Peru, and countless times in various North American universities, notably the University of California at Los Angeles, Princeton, Harvard, Stanford, Rice, Colorado at Boulder, Florida, and others. I have also taught courses like the one I gave at the University of Colorado on the Templo Mayor or the one at the University of Puerto Rico, where I spoke about archaeology in Mesoamerica. Also in the Universidad Complutense in Madrid and in Huelva. And in addition a three-month course in the École des Hautes Études en Sciences Sociales in Paris, substituting for my friend Jacques Soustelle.

There was a conference in Rome in 2004 in which numerous specialists participated, including the three of us. By coincidence, Leonardo López Luján was teaching a course at the Università L degli Studi de Roma ("La Spienza"), so he was able to organize that conference with the support of Alessandro Lupo and the Mexican Embassy.

Honors and recognitions

D: Why don't we talk a bit about your appointment as a member of the Colegio Nacional? What satisfaction has that brought you and how has it helped you to move forward with your plans?

E: From its inception, the Colegio Nacional has been thought of as equivalent to the French Academy, which included the most eminent individuals from the various fields of art, science, and the humanities. The members of the Colegio Nacional are considered the *Eméritos de la Nación*. It consists of forty members, and there were only two archaeologists: Don Alfonso Caso and Ignacio Bernal. Don Alfonso was a founding member in 1943. With the death of Ignacio Bernal, archaeology was no longer represented. Here I want to clarify something. If a post is vacant it doesn't necessarily have to be filled by a scholar from the same discipline. A specialist from any field whose accomplishments rise to an extraordinary level may be chosen. My name was proposed and I became a member in June, 1993. I gave a talk which I entitled "Tríptico del pasado" with the response given by the only woman who is a member of the Colegio Nacional, Dr. Beatriz de la Fuente.

Entering the Colegio Nacional was a great honor for me, since its membership includes people like Octavio Paz, Carlos Fuentes, Ramón Xirau, and José Emilio Pacheco; historians like Miguel León-Portilla, Silvio Zavala, and Luis González; artists like Vicente Rojo; astronomers like Arcadio Poveda and Manuel Peimbert, in short very outstanding people in various fields of knowledge and creativity. We meet once a month to transact the business of the institution and to share a meal.

D: Was there a celebration the day of your becoming a member?

E: My speech on entering was presided over by the writer José Emilio

Pacheco, who was the president that term. The ceremony took place at the Colegio which is almost across from the Templo Mayor. It is an old building with three patios inside. After a few words from the president, I gave my lecture. The presidium included the secretary of Public Education representing the president of the Republic; the rector of UNAM, José Sarukhán, also a member of the Colegio; the director of the Instituto Politécnico Nacional; and Rafael Tovar y de Teresa who was then president of the Consejo Nacional para la Cultura y las Artes. When my speech was finished, there was the response, which in this case was given by Dr. Beatriz de la Fuente, an outstanding scholar of pre-hispanic art, and a good friend. Afterward we walked over to a marvelous colonial house restored by the López Negretes which was near the Templo Mayor. José Luis Lorenzo, Lorena Mirambell, Mari Carmen Serra, and others were among the archaeologists who came.

The wine flowed generously . . . good wine, of course, and we had a great time.

D: Speaking of wine, what is your favorite?

E: It depends on the circumstances. I lean toward French wines like the Côtes du Rhone or the loveable Beaujolais, but I also like Italian wines like Valpolicella or Spanish wines like Marqués de Cáceres. As a rule I don't drink many Mexican wines, but that's not from a lack of patriotism.

D: What other honors do you remember?

E: I received one interesting honor at the headquarters of the Centro de Arqueología in Ravello, Italy. I was given the high honor of delivering the opening address at the conference on the beginnings of the excavations at Pompey and Herculaneum. That is the beginning of classical archaeology, and the conference was celebrating its 250 years of existence. Just imagine opening a conference on the classical archaeology of Europe with a talk on the Templo Mayor of Tenochtitlan! I was afraid this might not be very pleasing to the Italian archaeologists but it went very well. I was invited to participate by my good friend Dr. Jacques Soustelle.

I remember with great fondness being awarded the degree of Doctor Honoris Causa by the University of Colorado in Boulder in 1989. You were one of the people who brought that about. In order to award that degree, the University had to solicit the opinions of various specialists. Paul Wheatley, Doris Heyden, and other outstanding scholars offered very kind praises. I had participated in various conferences and courses in Boulder, and we had created the Mesoamerican Archive. All of this contributed to my being awarded that degree.

L: Tell us about other recognitions you have received for your work in archaeology.

E: I have always heard other people say that honors should be given to the living. And you know, it is very stimulating and gratifying to have your contributions recognized however great or small they may be. The first honor that comes to mind besides those we've already talked about was when I was notified by the cultural attaché of the German Embassy that the German Archaeological Institute had made me an honorary member. This was in 1988. One day the attaché came to my office, he stood there very ceremoniously, so I had to stand up too. Then he said a few words to me in German, which I didn't understand at all. Then he gave me a diploma in Latin, which I didn't understand either. He read me the diploma and handed it to me. He turned on his heel and marched out. This emotional ceremony lasted two minutes, and he and I were the only people present!

As far as diplomas and medals, I have three honors conferred by France: the Academic Palms by the Universities of France, the National Order of Merit, and Knight of Arts and Literature by the French Government. These were all given me around 1981 or 1982. I received the Orden Andrés Bello in 1988 along with Víctor Flores Olea, Arturo Azuela, and Jorge Carpizo. I was also named an Honorary Member of the Archaeological Institute of America in 1992.

I was named by my own institution, the INAH, as Profesor Emérito de Investigación Científica in 2000. The following year the auditorium of the Museo Templo Mayor was given my name. It was a simple ceremony. One very moving experience was receiving the Henry B. Nicholson Medal for excellence in research in Mesoamerican Studies from Harvard University. This was in 2002, and I say it was moving because it took place in the Peabody Museum, with its great tradition in Mesoamerican studies. Both Davíd Carrasco and Nicholson himself delivered very beautiful speeches. The dinner in the rooms of the museum was attended by many friends who came from Mexico: César Roel and his wife Gilda, Nacho Durán and his wife Lucero. I was accompanied by my present companion Gabriela. It was really unforgettable.

Another tribute which I found very moving took place in October of 2003 in the Museo Nacional de Antropología. It was organized by the INAH and Harvard University. The organizing committee was made up of Miguel León-Portilla, Alfredo López Austin, Beatriz de la Fuente, Manuel Ramos Medina, Felipe Solís, and Davíd Carrasco, but the greater part of the work was done by Leonardo López Luján and Lourdes Cué. There were five days of lectures given by both Mexican and foreign colleagues who were invited to participate. I was reunited with such friends as William Sanders, Elizabeth Boone, Henry Nicholson, Saburo Sugiyama, and many others who enriched the event with their presence. This was very important to me because they are my friends, I have known them for years, and what's more, I admire the work they have done. I consider them great masters of anthropology and of Mexican archaeology.

The response by younger colleagues was also important. Among them I should mention the presence of many members of the Templo Mayor project, young people who have had an important role in that research. There were also many Mexican scholars, friends and people whom I admire greatly such as Beatriz de la Fuente, Miguel León-Portilla, Alfredo López Austin, Felipe Solís, José Rubén Romero, Rubén Cabrera, Alejandro Pastrana, Guadalupe Mastache, Mari Carmen Serra, and so many more it would be impossible to name them all. In short they were all there sharing their knowledge. Dr. Teresa Uriarte, the Director of the Instituto de Investigaciones Estéticas, spoke on behalf of the Rector of UNAM. In the vestibule of the museum there was an exhibit which showed part of my academic life. It included my field notebooks and, of course, one of my pipes.

Toward the future . . .

L: What are the activities that you are presently engaged in, the projects you are working on, the books you are writing, your plans for the future?

E: Right now I am working on several books on subjects I have dealt with throughout my career. I am working on a *Historia de la arqueología en Mesoamérica* which is very far along, but has been delayed for various reasons. Even so, I have kept my hand in and we were able to put together the exposition "Descubridores del pasado en Mesoamérica" in the Colegio de San Ildefonso.

Another book I'm going to write is a general summary of the excavations and research from the Templo Mayor. As you know, to date around thirty professional theses have been presented, at all levels—Bachelor's, Master's, and PhD—and a number have received national and international prizes. The time has come to reflect on this; it has been twenty-seven years since we began our work in that site. It is interesting to see that when we began we took certain approaches with a specific focus and particular techniques which have been changing over the years. In fact, the project is now in the hands of young scholars who are carrying out significant work with their own focus, their own sets of problems, and their own techniques. As I said on the day of the tribute in October of 2003, what I had to say about the Templo Mayor, I said at the time. Now the new generations of archaeologists and other specialists who continue studying the Templo Mayor have the floor. It is up to them to ratify or modify what we said many years ago. And in turn their work will be revised by future generations of archaeologists. That is science: what is accepted today will be rejected tomorrow. . . .

The third volume which I have planned deals with the subject of death in pre-hispanic Mexico. As you know, it is a subject I have written about throughout my life and I think it is worthwhile to dedicate some time to making a deeper study of it. That is how I will wrap up my research and perhaps, given the subject, my life as well.

Nevertheless, as always happens, other projects seem to come along. One of those projects is a pair of books which the Colegio de México and the Fondo de Cultura Económica have asked for. They will be part of a new series on pre-hispanic cities which begins with *Tenochtitlan, la ciudad,* which I have already turned in. It should be published also in 2006. The other is for the same series and will be entitled *Teotihuacan, la ciudad.*

Besides that, I keep giving lectures. I give an average of more than twenty lectures per year, which means roughly two each month, in addition to presentations of articles in books, which some authors ask me for. The subjects of my talks include death, the Templo Mayor, the history of archaeology, Teotihuacan, and many others.

So, I continue with these projects, I keep publishing a lot, which I really love, and participating in conferences. Maybe someday I'll die writing. . . .

D: From the perspective of feelings, how has your life gone so far?

E: Significant changes have taken place. In 1995 I separated from María Luisa (la Bruja) with whom I lived for nearly seventeen years. This decision was made in large part by a beautiful woman. One day she appeared in my path and we began a relationship which only ended when, after anxiously savoring her skin and exploring her body inch by inch, she felt compelled to return to the bosom of her family.

It also happened that one fine day, before giving a lecture in the Museo Nacional de Antropología, I saw another woman enter the vestibule with a firm step and dignified carriage. She attracted my attention immediately, so much so that when we were introduced I remembered her name. When the lecture ended she headed for the exit and I followed her immediately. I caught up with her and said: "Gabriela, there is something I would like to tell you."

She turned around and I imagine it must have caught her attention that I remembered her name although we had just been introduced recently. I told her that I wanted to send her a book that I had written and hoped she would find it interesting. She gave me her telephone number and address and I sent her *The Face of Death*. I signed it with a message which she found striking, as she told me later. I finally married Gabriela in 1998, and am still living with her now. She is an intelligent and successful woman. I admire her in many ways.

Fig 42. Eduardo Matos in Madrid, Spain, 1981.

Fig 43. Alfredo López Austin, Eduardo Matos, and Ezequiel Ezcurra at the Templo Mayor.

Fig 44. Hunter Rawlings III, Davíd Carrasco, John Hoag, Lois Middleton, President E. Gordon Gee, and Eduardo Matos, visiting the Tlatelolco excavation sponsored, in part, by the University of Colorado's Moses Mesoamerican Archive.

Fig 45. Matos with Salvador Guilliem, who excavated in Tlatelolco under Eduardo's supervision. This project was carried out with funds raised by Davíd Carrasco from the University of Colorado, Boulder.

Fig 46. Longtime collaborators Johanna Broda, Eduardo Matos, and Alfredo López Austin.

Fig 47. Matos directing the excavation of the Pyramid of the Sun in Teotihuacan, 1993.

Fig 48. With Antonio Ariza, Pedro Ramírez Vázquez, and Rafael Tovar y de Teresa, president of the National Council for Culture and the Arts, at Teotihuacan, 1994.

Fig 49. Conference on Teotihuacan at the National Museum of Anthropology 2003.

Fig 50. Eduardo Matos in the Museum of the Templo Mayor. The Eagle Warrior looms behind him.

Fig 51. Becoming a member of the Mexican Society of History and Geography.

Fig 52. Eduardo Matos is named Emeritus Professor in the National Institute of Anthropology and History at a ceremony held in the National Museum of Anthroplogy in Mexico City, November 2000.

Fig 53. Eduardo Matos photographed by his friend Gilda Roel, 2000.

Chapter Six

Toward the Encounter with Death

D: We have come to the fifth and final breaking point. It is interesting that the Aztecs also had five epochs in their cosmology and that their analysis of space has five dimensions, the fifth being the center. So it's not just the fifth in terms of chronology, but also marks an arrival at the center of the world because the fifth dimension is the most crucial. There is a correspondence between the process of your life and the Aztec cosmology.

E: Every human has to face the fifth breaking point: it is the encounter with death. In my life the presence of death has been very significant. The first book I wrote was called *Death by Obsidian Knife*. I continued to develop the theme and published *The Face of Death*. Death is a unique experience that we only live once. Every other experience you can repeat. The experience of death you cannot. So I reiterate: death is the only experience we can have only once. Therefore we have to know how to live it, we have to know how to live death. We have to know how to face it, and this is where the measure of a person will be taken. This breaking point will be faced sooner or later.

So, how do we face it? How do we accomplish it? This is the problem that confronts humankind. One way is to create other worlds to which we will go after death. Many religions are involved in this. Humanity does not want to die and therefore invents the afterlife. I believe that what your life has been leads up to the way you will confront death. This reality of death is something that cannot be avoided. It is always said that Mexicans live with death, play with it, and so on. I think that is false. What I can tell you is that for me death is always present. I don't want to say that I consider myself attracted to death; on the contrary, I am a lover of life. I mean, my aim in life has always been to live this life fully in all its profundity, its greatness, its afternoons, its music, its fine wines, its troubles. In short, to live it all.

For myself, I do not believe in these other worlds. I don't believe in the hereafter. I don't believe in heavens or hells. I have talked about them. I like to write about them, above all what they imply about the thinking of ancient or modern peoples. But really I don't believe that any of that exists. I don't believe in gods or demons. This makes the confrontation with the final breaking point more difficult, because believers have this hope: "I am going to die, but I will then go to heaven or hell." They think of that other life. I don't think of it, for me there is no afterlife. I believe in myself. I believe in humanity. That's why I say: "The gods have not created mankind. . . . It is humans who have created the gods in their own image."

So then, since I think that way about death, in reality I am faced with something that ends there. At the moment of death everything will end, there won't be anything more. So, what happens? What has value in that death which is inevitably approaching is what one has done in one's life. If you have lived your life according to your principles, if you have sought a deep understanding of what life is, then you will know how to confront death. You will face it from your own perspective, knowing that there will not be an afterlife, knowing that everything will end there very consciously, and you will be able to live that final experience. There is the contradiction: one must know how to "live" death.

D: "One must know how to live death." I remember that one of my teachers, Paul Wheatley from the University of Chicago, once called me to tell me that a colleague of his was dying, and he said, "but that man is prepared for death." And I asked him why. "Because he was a teacher of the classics, of the great books of Aristotle, of Plato." And according to Wheatley, that is the importance of reading the classics, to prepare oneself for death, because they all deal with that question. Another time, at a dinner, I remember well that you were talking about different ways of dying. I know that you were talking half in jest, but you mentioned intentional death. Could you share some of your thoughts about that?

E: This has to do with two possibilities: whether death will come whenever it comes, by way of sickness or accident, or whether you are able, or willing, to determine the moment of your death. The second alternative gives you complete freedom, it is the ultimate power that one has at any given moment. I mean, one can decide to leave life and do so at a time of one's choosing. Remember, for example, the great Mexican poet Jaime Torres Bodet. Don Jaime had an incurable disease, but he was a very conscious man, and so he made the decision to commit suicide, to take his own life. He wrote some wonderful notes in which he said, "Rather than wait for death to come, I prefer to summon it and do it at the right time." And he shot himself. I admire Jaime Torres Bodet, and I mentioned him in my book *Death by Obsidian Knife*. In the final chapter I quoted this thought of his where he signed these words. It's like the person who has known how to live, who has contributed something, arrives at a moment when he also decides to end it. Many say that suicide is cowardice. Well, I believe that it is a cowardice only brave people commit.

My internal thoughts about this are these: "I am a man of the twentieth century. This is my century, the next will not be. In the twenty-first century I will be an old man, more than sixty years old.

I have given what I was able to give, for better or worse, and I might be able to contribute something more, but in reality, I think that all my experience is or was in the twentieth century."

Earlier, I decided to end my life on the 31st of December 2000. How would I do it? Well, we could return once more to ritual. Invite all my friends to the Templo Mayor, have them participate in the ritual and then die listening to classical music, for example that crowning moment in Beethoven's Chorale when the chorus enters and sings of the Elysian fields. I talked about this once with my psychoanalyst and told him: "What do you think of that idea? Because that part about gathering all one's friends might seem pathological to some people."

And he sat looking at me after I had told him all that, and he answered me: "No, I think that would be the perfect death for you."

To die with one's friends, at a great feast, toasting with the best French champagne. Then to calmly drop the substance that will take your life into that champagne. And to measure it so carefully that at the stroke of twelve, when the twenty-first century enters, at the final stroke, to remain trapped in my own time. . . .

Fig 54. Eduardo excavates the skullrack altar decorated with skulls on the north side of the Templo Mayor in 1980.

Fig 55. Eduardo at the Museum of the Great Temple in 1996. This photo was taken by his friend Gilda Roel.

Postscript

I DIDN'T KEEP MY WORD. Throughout the year 2000 I prepared my farewell ceremony, as Simone de Beauvoir called it, writing about Jean Paul Sartre. I watched evenings fall in the Templo Mayor and went to the restaurants I used to frequent during the years of excavations to evoke those times, but I didn't put my idea into practice. I saw the result one day in the mirror: a mature man, without hair, with a beard that is whitened by time. The body is not what it was years ago, and the doctors appear more often than one would like. The "red lights" begin to come on, and unexpected things happen. They find me to have unsuspected illnesses, and the number of analyses and pills grows day by day.

Painful events also begin to occur more frequently. One of them was the death of my son Eduardo in an automobile accident. Others, more recently, were the deaths of some collaborators in archaeological work who were younger than I. That was the case with Guadalupe Mastache and with Ana María Crespo. Here and there bombs fall that strike others, and cause you to crouch down to avoid being hit.

I have a much greater appreciation of friends now. I share some very happy times with them, and the same is true with family. I see my siblings often, and Daniela has given me three granddaughters. Rainer is fifteen, plays the piano, and is a good student. He seems to want to study history. We have taken some wonderful trips with Gabriela to France, Spain, Italy, England, Greece, and the Caribbean. In fact on our first trip to Paris in 1995, we went to visit Notre Dame. It was in the afternoon when the sun was declining and shone in through the stained glass windows with a marvelous light. We sat to listen to the silence, and suddenly, a choir could be heard through the afternoon and the sunlight. Everything was transformed. Those voices penetrated the walls into the most hidden parts of the stonework and one's being. A unique experience that brings us close to the angels . . . even though we don't believe in them . . .

Gabriela represents the positive, vital side of my life. One day she told me, referring to the house we built together: We worked hard to build this house. It is completely full of life. In the patio there is a fountain, there are singing birds and growing plants. . . . Every corner is ours.

I live intensely morning and afternoon. I write books and articles which are requested of me from various quarters. I travel with some frequency to give lectures both in Mexico and in other countries. I exercise daily to "stay in shape." Even so, I keep thinking that I let the moment for acting on the fifth breaking point go by. Now I pay the price in front of the mirror, although—why deny it?—I also enjoy the pleasures of life.

So, I have not settled my debt with death. I will have to wait for that moment to come. Maybe it no longer depends on me. In any case, I live with it daily when I write about the past. My work causes me to confront dead eras and bring them back to life. On one occasion I wrote the following: "The journey we begin today will permit us to do two things: to go back several centuries in this modern time machine we call archaeology, since the archaeologist is permitted to recuperate time by means of excavations; and further, to arrive at the world of the dead, where we find the faces of those who once lived, who look at us with stony eyes across time itself."

Estoy listo. I am ready. . . .

Pensamientos

My Testament
To my daughter Daniela

When I am ashes
you will inherit my body . . .
That's all I can leave you
I have nothing more.
You'll inherit my afternoons
you'll inherit the wind
you'll inherit my flesh
you'll inherit my breath.
I will leave you my poems
with a scrap of time. . . .
My anguish will be yours
my memories, yours.
That's all I can leave you
I have nothing more.
I will leave you my autumns
with all the leaves falling. . . .
And when you are with me
when I shall have died,
then you will be wealthy,
you'll have inherited the wind,
the evenings, the poppies
the rain, the air, and thunder
the blue lightning
and the milky moon.

I cannot leave you gold
because I have no gold.
I have in my pockets
only a scrap of time.
You will not blame me,
because I leave you everything
a little white snow
a lot of ancient time
an afternoon rain
my long beard flowing
my ageless sadness
my incurable loneliness
my old, hot pipe
my young, prophetic tears.
I will leave you wealthy;
you will inherit time:
That's all I can leave you
I have nothing more.
When the notary inscribes
his signature on the document
then you will be very rich:
You will have inherited time. . . .

ALABAMA

Alabama. . . .
Your streets are rivers
Of red waters
Black bodies
With white entrails.
Alabama. . . .
Your curse spreads out
Across the brown land
Filling the blue waters
With blood
Alabama. . . .
Those black bodies
With white entrails
Form a red star
Upon the waters.

—April 1965, on the murder
of Negroes in Alabama.

TO CUBA

Sister Cuba
plays the bongo
dances rumba
prays to Changó.
Cuts the cane,
Sweating, sweating
The blacks all sing
Suffering sings.
Bitter is the sugar
Sugar of the oppressor
The sugar of freedom

Is sweeter by far
The star now shines
Without fear
No longer alone
It has color!
The maracas sound
The bongo breaks in
Let the black woman dance
Who prays to Changó. . . .

—1965

I Come From a Beautiful Distant Country

I come from a beautiful distant country
with millennial red suns.
I come from the dawn and the dew,
I bring the sweet violin note of summer.
A yellowed leaf in the filtering light
of a red sun's afternoon setting.
I am the sad, gray dawn,
the unknown clarity in emptiness.
I come from a country beautiful, distant,
Cold. . . . .
When evening falls with its soft melody
I am the tenuous light over all,
the wan trees without green life.
The mist arrives with its calm grayness,
penetrates and covers the brown, broken flesh
with robes dyed purple.
I am the evening. . . . .
The leaves fall softly
swept along for life by the wind
they move aimless through the evening
toward a beautiful distant country.
The gray, the evening, the autumn and its leaves.
I am a beautiful distant country. . . . .

How Sad and Lovely Is Solitude

How sad and lovely is solitude.
Green stains vibrating against red,
Above, the gray of the mist falling,
falling . . .
I want to think but can't
philosophize on life,
and I so love freedom
that the fine weave of the window screen
seems like prison bars to me,
and I despair. . . .

—Malpaso, Chiapas, January 23, 1966

Erectario

I

We have formed a perfect communicant vessel:
You feed me on your essence of woman,
As I spill into your mouth
The life that escapes me fleeting . . .

II

There are three paths that lead inside you:
The first is damp and tastes of red wine.
The other leads me through a forest of leafless trees
and tastes of white wine.
The third has acacia leaves
tastes of rosé.
I wander all three through endless afternoons
I drink them from an infinite glass. . . .

III

One day I wandered aimless across your skin
when I came to a corner of your body and stopped.
I peered cautiously and saw a path with no end,
which took me to your innermost essence.

IV

My tongue began to wander to the most hidden part of your body
And came at last to rest in your mouth.
Since then I say that you are made of wine, sweat, tears . . .
and of a little evening mixed with melancholy,
and a faint trace of time . . .

V

Your body is a solitary land:
there are woodlands, valleys,
there are enchanted grottoes and clear fountains.
There are parts which grow and others which tremble.
There is all that spurs the search for lost Eden. . . .

—Paris, autumn of 1981

Capturing time

One day I stood at the window of time. I found ancient faces, eyes
that saw me through obsidian crystal and oceanic eyes. I saw the
knife that brings death—death by obsidian knife—the caracol, which
brings life. I looked upon the faces of life and death. I could stop time
with my hands, with my beard . . . the time I sought for years, which
captured me in time, past, the time captured, in all times. I returned
to the past and gave it life; the past repaid me, too, giving me a part
of itself. That's why I have an old man's beard, an old man's baldness
and childish tears. I returned, as Proust said "in search of lost time"
. . . I recovered it so that today's youths might also recover the incor-
poreal, might live it, might transcend it . . . Afterward we'll return to
time to stay, with an empty gaze, seeing pass before us the faces that
will have to rescue us from lost time in another thousand years . . .

The Face of Life . . . and of Death

Caracol is the symbol of life.
The artist who shaped it not only created life through its form
But melded volume and rhythm and formed,
In softly spreading lines,
The constant, endless motion of the living symbol.
In its infinite beauty,
the caracol speaks to us of water, sea, rain, fertility . . .
in all, all that makes up life. . . .
. . . . and death
The constant, perennial presence of the face of death.
With the sacrifice of the man-god comes the thirst for blood,
precious liquid—semen of the gods—which united with bone—
the dead element—brings life to the universe, the gods,
      humanity . . .
A cult of death? No, a cult of life. . . . through death. . . .

Chronology

1940—Eduardo is born December 11 in Mexico City. His parents are Rafael Matos Díaz, diplomat, and Edith Moctezuma Barreda, housewife.

1941—Eduardo, his parents, his brother Rafael, and his grandmother María Barreda de Moctezuma travel to Panama in the ship "América" because his father is to serve there as a diplomat. His sister María Fernanda is born one year later in Panama.

1943—Rafael Matos Díaz is transferred to Venezuela as Ambassador from the Dominican Republic.

1945—Diplomatic relations between Venezuela and the Dominican Republic are broken off after the attack on the Embassy where the Matos family lived. They return to Santo Domingo, Dominican Republic.

1946—Rafael Matos is named Ambassador to Panama. Eduardo attends school at the Colegio Miramar, of the La Salle Brothers through the third year of primary school.

1950—Rafael Matos is named Ambassador to Honduras. They live in Tegucigalpa until 1952, when Rafael Matos resigns the post on account of political differences with the Dominican dictator, Rafael Trujillo Molina.

1952—They return to Mexico. Eduardo studies at the Escuela Inglesa para Varones and later at the Instituto Patria, under the Jesuits, where he finishes primary school.

1954–1956—Eduardo attends secondary school at the Instituto Alonso de la Veracruz, under the Augustines. He breaks with religion.

1957–1958—Eduardo studies at the Colegio Cristóbal Colón.

1959—Eduardo enters the Escuela Nacional de Antropología e Historia to study archaeology. In the first semester his teachers are José Luis Lorenzo, Calixta Guiteras, Moisés Romero, and Jorge Vivó. The Cuban Revolution is victorious.

1960–1961—Eduardo enters the Instituto Nacional de Antropología e Historia as an intern in Historical and Geographical Sciences. He continues his studies and begins his fieldwork with Professor José Luis Lorenzo in Tepeapulco and Richard MacNeish in Tehuacan. Travels to Bonampak with Raúl Pavón Abreu. He works under Román Piña Chan in Comalcalco. He participates in salvage excavations in Tlatelolco under the direction of Francisco González Rul.

1962–1964—The Teotihuacan Project is carried out under the direction of Ignacio Bernal. Eduardo works under the direction of Jorge Acosta in the Palace of the Butterflies and is entrusted with the excavation of the Palace of the Plumed Snails. In 1964 he is assigned Zone 9 of the Street of the Dead. Toward the end of 1964 he carries out the salvage excavation of a small Aztec *adoratorio* in the Calle de Argentina, and collaborates with the German Foundation for Scientific Research with Dr. Bodo Spranz on the work at Totemihuacan, in Puebla.

1965—Eduardo graduates from UNAM as Master of Anthropological Sciences and Archaeologist of the Secretary of Public Education, with the paper "La revolución urbana en la Cuenca de México." His advisory committee is: President, Pedro Bosch Gimpera; members: Julio César Olivé, Arturo Romano, and Leonardo Manrique, and Secretary, Noemí Castillo.

1966—Eduardo works in salvage archaeology in Malpaso, Chiapas, with Carlos Navarrete and members of the New World Archaeological Foundation, including Gareth Lowe, Thomas Lee, and Pierre Agrinier. On his return he becomes supervisor of field work at Project Cholula, under the direction of Miguel Messmacher.

1967—Eduardo leaves the Project Cholula on account of a disagreement between the project's managers and the authorities led by Alfonso Caso, Ignacio Bernal, Jorge Acosta, and José Luis Lorenzo. This involves a generational struggle between two positions within the field of anthropology, specifically in archaeology. He is named associate director of Pre-hispanic Monuments.

1968—The antigovernment student movement arises. Eduardo marries María Eugenia del Valle Prieto with whom he has two children: Eduardo and Daniela. Dr. Ignacio Bernal assumes the directorship of the INAH upon the death of Dr. Eusebio Dávalos. Eduardo teaches various courses in the ENAH where he remains a professor for more than 30 years.

1971—Eduardo is named as director of the ENAH, which he directs until 1973. During those years he serves along with Jaime Litvak as the secretary of the Sociedad Mexicana de Antropología.

1972—Eduardo coordinates the Tula Project with the collaboration of Guadalupe Mastache, Ana María Crespo, and Juan Yadeun.

1974—Eduardo travels to the People's Republic of China along with Guillermo Bonfil, Román Piña Chan, and other scholars. In November he travels to Moscow and Kiev, where he gives lectures.

1975—Eduardo is named director of Pre-hispanic Monuments by Dr. Guillermo Bonfil.

1976—Eduardo serves as a member of the commission for the study of Ichcateopan.

1977—Gastón García Cantú names Eduardo president of the Council of Archaeology.

1978—Eduardo is named coordinator of the Templo Mayor project, a post he holds until the present day. In this period he renews contact with Davíd Carrasco, with whom he coordinates the meetings which will be held in following years in Boulder, Colorado.

1978–1982—The excavations of the Templo Mayor are carried out. Various studies on the subject are published.

1981—Eduardo is awarded the Academic Palms by the Universities of France.

1982—Eduardo is named by the President of the Republic as general director of the Centro de Investigaciones y Estudios Superiores en Antropología Social (CIESAS), a post in which he remains until 1986. He receives the National Order of Merit from the Republic of France. Also the title of Knight of Arts and Literature from the French Cultural Ministry.

1986—Eduardo is named by the Secretary of Public Education to the directorship of the National Museum of Anthropology.

1987—Eduardo requests a transfer to the directorship of the Museum of the Templo Mayor, inaugurated in October of this year. He holds this post until 2001.

1989—Eduardo's son Rainer María is born. Eduardo is named Doctor Honoris Causa in Science by the University of Colorado at Boulder.

1991—Eduardo founds the Programa de Arqueología Urbana (PAU) which has continued to the present day.

1992–1994—The Proyecto Especial Teotihuacan, coordinated by Eduardo, is begun. The new museum on the site is built. Eduardo founds the Centro de Estudios Teotihuacanos with the Scholarship Program. He excavates around the Pyramid of the Sun, and names Rubén Cabrera to head the salvage archaeology work in La Ventilla.

1995—Eduardo separates from María Luisa, "La Bruja."

1998—Eduardo marries Gabriela Galindo y Villa on April 4, in Mexico City.

1999—Eduardo's son Eduardo dies in an automobile accident.

2000—Eduardo is named an Emeritus Professor of the INAH.

2001—The auditorium at the Templo Mayor is named in Eduardo's honor.

2002—He is awarded the Henry B. Nicholson Medal by Harvard University for excellence in research in Mesoamerican studies. Gabriela and various friends accompany him in the ceremony and honorary dinner in the rooms of the Peabody Museum.

2003—From the 20th to the 24th of October of this year the Jornadas Académicas en honor de Eduardo Matos are held in the Museo Nacional de Antropología. This event is organized by the INAH and Harvard University, with the participation of about fifty national and international scholars. An exhibit of photographs, books, and honors is mounted in the vestibule of the museum.

2004—The Secretary of Culture of the Distrito Federal honors Eduardo on the door frame of the Feria del Libro in the Zócalo in Mexico City.

Index

Page Numbers in italic text indicate illustrations